Dear Mary Jo,

May the Chutz#
be with you!

Love,

Dlora
6-2-01

The Chutzpah*
Connection

The Chutzpah* Connection

Connection

BLUEPRINT FOR SUCCESS
Real Life Stories
of Inspiration
and Achievement

* chutz´pah (khûts´pə) *n. (Colloq.)*
boldness, nerve, courage, gall,
gumption, and audacity.

Idora Silver

CHUTZPRESS
3855 PICCADILLY DRIVE, RENO, NEVADA 89509

The Chutzpah* Connection

Blueprint for Success

Real Life Stories of
Inspiration and Achievement

© Copyright 1996, Idora Silver

Library of Congress Card Number: 96-68690

ISBN: 0-9652582-0-3

10 9 8 7 6 5 4 3 2

Published in association with Conscious Books
Reno, Nevada 1-800-322-9943.

Cover design by Paul Cirac

Designed at White Sage Studios
Drawer G, Virginia City, Nevada 89440

Printed and bound in Singapore
by Tien Wah Press

Contents

PART III

Acknowledgments

WE TRAVEL THIS LIFE ALONE. Or do we? None of us can truly be successful without help from others.

This is a change-of-life book for me. I began writing it as I started going through certain physical and emotional changes, which included reevaluating what was truly important in life. One definitely important aspect was the positive influence my friends and family have had on me. I am so blessed. Both the family I was born into and the families I have formed mean the world to me. Writing this book became a catharsis for a woman finishing one phase of her life and moving into another.

Whatever I am today is greatly due to the people included in this book and others. I know I do not thank you enough. Let this book be a tribute to you who have meant so much to me.

I am sure many of you do not even know how much you have helped me overcome obstacles in my life. I hope the readers of this book will get the same strength from your stories that I have.

First, thanks to the people in my book who have so graciously allowed me to interview them, hear their stories, and then present the stories in my own way. To my dear friends Kathleen Dickinson, Kathleen Maraden, Patty Gerken, and Patty Arnott, thank you for always being there and for making me laugh. To Bill and Maureen Eng; one helps me with my accounting and the other with my writing. Who could ask for a better duet of encouragement. To Lynn Williams and Dr. Ditto, your help and encouragement have been invaluable. To Chris Gant who gave me the final impetus to write this book, I hope you like it. To my mentors in life, Bob Byrd, Del Snider, and John Dooley; each of you in your own way has helped me believe in myself at times when even I did not.

To my family members, Sam and Sylvia, Arvin and JoAnn, Adella, Barclay, Brandan, Spencer, and, of course, Gus and Milt; you are all so special.

To John and Margaret Silver for being great other parents to John, Jr., and for encouraging me through these many years.

To Marilyn Lindesmith, my friend and my typist; there isn't a thing I have done in the last eleven years that could have been done without your patience, persistence, intelligence, and consistency. What a chutzy lady you are.

To my speaking partners, Tom Kubistant, Ed.D, and Valerie Wiener, M.A., M.A.; you are like soul mates to me. The inspiration I get from each of you continues to move me to my next level. Thank God for our "depression dinners."

And finally, to son John; you are almost grown now. I have learned a great deal about life while trying to teach you. Rearing you has given me the most profound joy. None of my successes in life would be important were it not for sharing them with you.

To all of you mentioned above, and others too numerous to list, I love all of you and thank you for nudging me to write this book.

Introduction

WRITING A BOOK ON CHUTZPAH is an interesting adventure and, as I have discovered, takes great chutzpah. I first thought that I would like to tell the stories of well-known heroes, so I developed a letter and interview survey form which I sent to a number of people throughout the world. A few wrote back or had their secretaries respond to say that they thought the idea was a good one, but that they were unable at this time to contribute. These people included Ted Turner, Oliver North, General Chuck Yeager, Elizabeth Taylor, Helen Gurley Brown, Lady Di (the Princess of Wales), Phyllis Diller, Steven Spielberg, President Clinton, Leona Helmsley (see section on over-chutzpah), and Vice President Al Gore. One of my graduate school professors wrote that it sounded like an interesting book idea, but that "the notion of chutzpah as an internal cause of or explanation for observable behaviors is a bit too mentalistic for me." Whatever that meant.

A number of others either did not respond or were not at the address to which I sent the request. These included Red Adair, Erma Bombeck, James & Sarah Brady, Chevy Chase, Billy Crystal, John DeLorean, Alan Dershowitz, Jane Fonda, Whoopi Goldberg, Pope John Paul II, Lee Iacocca, Larry King, Steven King, Mother Teresa, Geraldo Rivera, Joan Rivers, Dr. Ruth Westheimer, Eunice Kennedy Shriver, Richard Simmons, Gloria Steinem, Barbara Streisand, Barbara Walters, Robin Williams, Oprah Winfrey, Jim Abbott, Jackie Joyner-Kersee, Greg Louganis, Madonna, Mary Lou Retton,

Donald Trump, and Mike Tyson.

A formidable list. What was I to do now? Well, the only thing left was to talk to real people. Real people who knew me and who would take the time to share their life experiences with me for a book on chutzpah. So the book took a definite turn. Instead of recounting the lives of people we all know, I decided to write the book about regular people who are less-known, but who have achieved something outstanding within the framework of a more ordinary life. Like yours. Like mine.

My friends have been my inspiration for years. They have stood by me, encouraged me, and made me laugh even when I didn't think there was anything to laugh about. To all of you, I say thank you. This book is about you and for you.

Dedication

To Uncle Gus and Uncle Julie –
A Hearty 4-Finger Salute!

Part I

Chutzpah and Success

1

Chutzpah

My grandmother's name was Ida. She came to this country around the turn of the century, a poor but proud immigrant woman. She arrived with two distinctive traits. One was her talent for sewing. She had great pride in her ability to make her own clothes. One day in 1906 she was sporting a beautiful, homemade outfit with eyelet cuffs, collar, waistband, and layers of full skirts. She carried a matching parasol and wore shoes with matching buttons. She sported this new ensemble to the train station to greet her sister. But as she walked toward the train, she felt that something wasn't quite right. And the more she walked, the more she felt something slip. It slipped, she walked. She walked, it slipped. She was gripped by terror when she realized that the waistband of her slip had given out and was working its way toward her feet. As she neared the train, the inevitable happened. The slip fell and collapsed around her ankles.

Now, in addition to my grandmother Ida's talent for sewing, she had one other trait – the ability to use "chutzpah." With her head held high, she stepped completely and confidently out of her slip, pretended nothing was wrong, and continued on to greet her sister!

This is a book about chutzpah and the need for people to use this trait to make themselves more successful. It tells the real life stories of people who have used chutzpah to achieve levels beyond which they had imagined possible in their personal and professional lives. It is a book about courage, boldness, assertiveness, rebellion, uppityness, and sometimes arrogance. It is about success.

Chutzpah is a Yiddish term for gall, brazen nerve, effrontery, incredible "guts," presumption, and arrogance. Attorney Alan Dershowitz, who wrote a book entitled *Chutzpah,* says, "Chutzpah is a concept more easily demonstrated than defined. We immediately recognize a chutzpahnik – that is, a person manifesting the quality of chutzpah – when we observe him or her in action, despite the inadequacy of single word definitions. Indeed, the word chutzpah has both a positive and negative connotation. To the perpetrator, chutzpah means boldness, assertiveness, a willingness to demand what is due, to defy tradition, to challenge authority, to raise eyebrows. To the victim of chutzpah, it means unmitigated gall, nerve, uppityness, arrogance, hypocritical, demanding. It is truly in the eye of the beholder."

The classic illustration of chutzpah describes the young man who murdered his parents and then begs the judge, "Please, Your Honor, have mercy on me for I am an orphan." Another illustration supplied by Leo Rostin in the book, *The Joys of Yiddish,* illustrates it thus: " A friend of mine swears that in a Jewish restaurant, he once asked the passing waiter, What time is it? Icily, the waiter said, You aren't my table." Alan Dershowitz goes further to describe chutzpah with the example of a client convicted of selling false antiques, who tries to pay him – in antiques! Dershowitz, himself, demonstrates chutzpah when, in his book, he includes the following footnote: "If you come across any other definitions or illustrations, please send them to me, c/o Harvard Law School, for inclusion in the next printing. Talk about chutzpah!"

A Good Thing

SOME OF YOU may be confused. Chutzpah has generally been thought of as a negative, presumptuous thing, like that exhibited by the cab driver I saw the other day driving the wrong way on a one-way street in busy downtown San Francisco, honking and yelling at everybody to get out of *his* way! But chutzpah can be positive in that it is assertive, demanding, and creative, and can be used to help people achieve at new levels in their lives.

A Bad Thing

WE MUST DISTINGUISH between chutzpah and *over-chutzpah* – being overly aggressive, mean, nasty, and selfish. Examples of people using over-chutzpah include Leona Helmsley when she allegedly said, "Only the little people pay taxes;" Imelda Marcos who thought her need for new shoes was more important than her countrypeople's need for food; Saddam Hussein who thought that a little *might* meant he could do anything he wanted; and, most recently, Colin Ferguson, the Long Island shooter who insisted on defending himself – and then said he was improperly tried because he lacked adequate counsel! These people are anti-heroes and have not achieved anything positive. Chutzpah is healthy for you. It gives you a strong ego, boosts your self-esteem, and helps you toward a life of self-empowerment, decreased stress, increased happiness, and a feeling of individuality and accomplishment.

Genetic or Learned?

WHILE THERE MAY BE a genetic predisposition to chutzpah, as some people seem to come by it naturally, the successful components of chutzpah can certainly be learned and developed. This book will teach you how to develop more chutzpah in order to get what you want and need out of life.

My Family

IN LOOKING AT the genetic involvement, I have seen plenty of chutzpah in my heritage. And it appears that in my family, chutzpah is passed down through the women. My mother, the daughter of Ida, went to the hospital some time ago for a very serious surgery. It was a procedure whereby the surgeon cuts into the ear and removes a growth. It is a very delicate operation for should he slip and nick the brain, then Mom wouldn't be Mom as we know her. The whole family was there to wish her well before the procedure, but when she was returned to her room a couple hours later, I was the only one there. When they wheeled Mom in, she looked pretty good, but was neither conscious nor speaking. I was anxious to know if she was okay.

"Mom, Mom. You there?"

"Hhhmmm," was her groggy response.

"Mom, anything I can do for you?"

"Hhhmmmmmm. Idora..."

"What, Mom, what?"

"Idora – I gotta pee."

"Oh, okay, Mom. Don't go anywhere. I'll go get the bedpan. Be right back." So I rushed to the nurse and returned with the shiny, bright bedpan.

"Mom," I said, "You're gonna have to roll over so I can slip this thing underneath you."

Without opening her eyes, without looking around, Mom whispered loudly to me, "Idora. Sit on it first and warm it for me!" Now, *that* was a chutzy lady. Even semi-conscious, she had chutzpah enough to demand her due. A loving daughter should be willing to warm up the bedpan before slipping it under her mother's tush.

My sister's son, nephew Spencer, seemed slow to grow, but also exhibited early signs of chutzpah. At the age of 12, he was taken to a specialist to be examined. Spencer had disrobed and was lying on the examining table with just a sheet covering him. The doctor was proceeding with the examination and at just about the point when he was going to examine my nephew's more private parts, Spencer reached his arm out, grabbed the doctor by the nose, and said, "Now, doctor, we're not going to hurt each other, are we?"

Chutzpah also helps us create inventive and decisive actions to other situations, as illustrated by my cousin Alan, a conscientious radiological technician in a large San Francisco hospital. Alan tells this story: "One day a physician at my hospital had just cast a broken lower leg. We were standing side-by-side looking at the after X-ray and noticed that it wasn't right. The doctor looked at his watch. It was about lunch time. He shrugged it off and started to walk away. I punched him hard on the shoulder. He reset the leg. Then we lunched together." Sometimes you just gotta do what you gotta do.

Chutzpah, then, can be used in a variety of ways to help us live more successfully – to protect our dignity, to stand up for ourselves, and, at times, to stand up for others. My friend Kathleen shares several examples from her life.

Kathleen

BORN TO A working class family of Irish immigrants, many of her relatives were opinionated, outspoken, and earthy. Kathleen claims that she has always had dignity, but has no idea where it came from.

"When I was about three years old, I woke up early one morning to go to the bathroom, but the ceiling was pouring down water. Undaunted, I went to the closet and retrieved my umbrella. I opened it, did my business, then closed the umbrella and put it away. I woke my mother and told her that it was raining in the bathroom. I then went back to bed."

In addition to helping her retain dignity, Kathleen has used chutzpah for survival.

"For many years, I worked for the government abroad. Beirut of 1975 was a dangerous place. I was being sent by my office to Germany for a few days of R & R. I was being driven to the Beirut airport by an embassy driver who had been a musician and a beautician. He was a kind, gentle man, but he had a nervous streak. We were about five miles from the airport when we were accosted at a roadblock by a dozen men with weapons. Some of the men started to hit the windshield with the butts of their guns. Samir, my driver, panicked. He could not move. I also should have been petrified, but instead I put my foot over his on the gas pedal, took the steering wheel in my hands, and quickly drove to the airport. I used a very chutzy move to save our lives."

Getting what we want and need out of life is what chutzpah is all about, even if it sometimes means raising our voices. In September 1977 Kathleen was in Doctor's Hospital in Washington, D.C. The doctor had just given her a very painful injection of antibiotic into her inflamed right eye, telling her a nurse would be along shortly to give her a shot of Demerol for the pain. Kathleen waited and waited. She pushed the intercom button and asked about the status of the shot. The nurse responded that she would be there in a minute. She waited, re-pushed the button, and again waited. She was in pain and not getting her needs met, so she screamed at the top of her lungs – just a very straightforward, shrill, bloodcurdling, unending scream. It was amazing how quickly she received her pain-relieving shot.

"I've also used chutzpah to put other people in their place when I felt they needed it, and it hasn't mattered who the person was. When I was only 20, I worked as a legal secretary for the summer. The senior partner was a conscientious attorney with integrity. The junior partner was arrogant. The junior partner came back from lunch one day in a foul mood and yelled to me to get in here and take dictation. I did not move. He yelled again. Get the hell in here and take this memo. I did not move. He came out, stood at my desk and rudely asked what I thought I was doing. I said, I will gladly come in and do what you want if you are polite and ask me with a *please.* Otherwise, I'm staying here to finish what I am doing. He went back to his office. When the senior partner came in, the junior told him what had happened. The senior partner sided with me and informed junior he was to be courteous to the staff at all times."

Chutzpah can, therefore, be used for maintaining dignity and poise, for getting your needs met, and sometimes for saving your life. Kathleen's next example illustrates how chutzpah can also be used to make a remarkable difference in this world for others.

"I was in my early 30's when my father was dying of cancer and in intractable pain. None of traditional medicine's pain relievers would help and the only thing left to him was the use of heroin. But, of course, heroin was illegal. I hated watching my father suffer. I hated the law which kept him from getting the relief that he needed. He would never approve of using an illegal drug or a drug in an illegal manner. So I went to Congress, testified, and lobbied for the Intractable Pain Relief Bill in 1984 and 1985 on behalf of my father."

Chutzpah Improves the World

THE WORLD HAS moved forward because of people who have had the unmitigated gall to pursue new frontiers and refuse to take "no" for an answer. Consider the advances made in travel by the chutzpah of the Wright Brothers and Henry Ford. And the advances in business by the chutzpah of Lee Iacocca when he demanded a loan from the Federal Government to keep the auto industry afloat.

Imagine the chutzpah of Roger Bannister who proved that a human being could beat the four-minute mile, of Rosa Parks for not giving up her seat, and of Jackie Robinson who became the first black athlete in major league baseball. Let's not forget the chutzpah of Branch Rickie, his white coach, who encouraged him to continue on. And remember the chutzpah of Thomas Jefferson, one of our country's founding fathers, who said that he believed all people were created equal and that we could form a government to represent that. A chutzy proclamation indeed from a man who himself owned slaves.

Imagine the chutzpah of Eleanor Roosevelt who was told she was much too homely to ever get a husband. Undaunted, she married, became first lady of the land, and went on to save millions of orphans in Europe after World War II. And the list goes on.

The world abounds with famous people who have used

chutzpah to achieve for themselves and to enhance their world. This book is only partially about famous people, however. It is a book primarily about ordinary people. People like you and me who have found the courage, gall, and even effrontery to pursue dreams, stand up for ourselves, stand up for others, achieve levels in our lives we had never dreamed of, and, of course, make the world a better place in which to live.

A few years ago, I started speaking to audiences about how to achieve their "field of dreams." The audiences loved hearing my stories of famous people, but also seemed to relate to my personal tales, many of which included chutzpah. So I decided to write this book.

In researching the lives of famous individuals and in interviewing my friends–the heroes in my own life whose stories are not public but who have made great advancements with nerve, gall, arrogance, presumption, and rebellion–I consistently found 10+ traits shared by most successful, chutzy people.

In the chapters that follow, each of these characteristics or traits will be described with an illustration from the lives of my friends. These personal stories give us lessons on how to become more successful in our own lives. From the lives of ordinary people who have done extraordinary things, we learn the advantages of using the chutzpah connection as a *blueprint for success.*

But First . . .

BEFORE WE BEGIN, you should first become familiar with your current level of chutzpah. The next chapter includes a self-assessment quiz. From your score, you will be able to determine your current chutzpah quotient and whether you need to increase it, decrease it, or steady the course. In any case, this book is for you. Read on.

2

Measuring Your Chutzpah Quotient (CHQ)

Real life gives us many opportunities to use chutzpah. As described, chutzpah is the assertion of one's needs and rights. It is creative and distinctive to the individual. It is used to retain poise in otherwise embarrassing or undignified situations, to put other people in their place, to overcome obstacles or barriers, and to help you achieve new levels of success.

The following questions will help you determine your current level of chutzpah. Answer the questions as they pertain to you in everyday and not-so-everyday situations. Be honest. The score is for your use only. So, what are you afraid of? Go ahead.

1. A person butts in front of you in line at the grocery store. You:

POINTS

1 ❑ a. Gently move back to make room.

3 ❑ b. Yell, "Line police – arrest that person! S/He has violated my shopping civil rights. I want action – now!"

2 ❑ c. Say, "Excuse me, but I was here in line ahead of you. Are you in a big hurry? Do you need to go before me?"

2. *You're leaving a fast food restaurant and see a young man throw his empty drink carton out of the car window onto the parking lot. You hate trash, so you:*

1 ❑ a. Drive away grumbling about the disrespect of the kids these days.

3 ❑ b. Get in your car and ram him – now he'll know how much you hate trash!

2 ❑ c. Walk over to the car, pick up the drink carton, and say, "Excuse me, but I think you dropped this. You look busy, so I will throw it away properly for you."

3. *All your life you were told you were adopted. One day you secretly discover that you are a true blood member of the family. You:*

1 ❑ a. Consider yourself a real outsider. Refuse to talk to your parents ever again.

3 ❑ b. Immediately confront your parents and accuse them of being blatant liars.

2 ❑ c. Bide your time. There must be a reason – you will find out and deal with it better later on.

4. *You survive a near-fatal car accident. After a long recovery, you have residual brain damage and cannot speak as fluently as before. You:*

1 ❑ a. Retreat into your personal shell. It's too embarrassing to go out and face the world with your disability.

3 ❑ b. Sue your employer for giving you a new, less stressful position. How dare they discriminate against a disabled person!

2 ❑ c. Become a motivational speaker. Tell groups of your struggles to help them overcome theirs. Let that shell become your oyster.

5. *You were reared on the wrong side of the tracks, but now you are a wealthy, successful industrialist. You:*

1 ❑ a. Keep quiet; give to needy others by sending corporate checks.

3 ❑ b. Live lavishly; after all, you have worked hard for all you have. Why help people who haven't helped you?

2 ❑ c. Set up an educational foundation to help needy, at-risk children. Give money and give time.

6. *As far as dreams go:*

1 ❑ a. I am afraid to dream. I've had too many disappointments in my life.

3 ❑ b. My dreams are no business of yours! Buzz off, Idora.

2 ❑ c. I have wonderful, exciting dreams for my future.

TOTAL SCORE: _____

Scoring

A LOW SCORE (6-11) means that you answered mostly a's and that you really need to develop more chutzpah. You are somewhat afraid of the world and its reaction to you. You have some insecurities about your ability to get what you need and allow others to step on you. STOP THIS IMMEDIATELY! You have every right to get what you need and to avoid people who stop you, slow you, insult you, or in any other way impede your progress. Start using the 10+ traits in your own life. They will help you be more successful in attaining your goals.

Score around 12: You have chutzpah and are probably quite successful. You are comfortable with yourself and are caring, yet assertive. You do not hurt people, but you speak up for yourself and for others. I know you will thoroughly enjoy reading the stories of other chutzy people described in this book. Perhaps you will learn a few notions to help you achieve at even higher levels of success.

Score over 12: OVER CHUTZPAH ALARM! Too much gall. Have you been accused of being rude, boorish, or aggressive? Be careful. In order to be successful, you need to regard the needs of others as well as your own. You need to find more creative ways to stand up for yourself. Read this book. You will find a number of examples from creative, chutzy people who have achieved a great deal in their lives without sacrificing the needs and feelings of others.

Let's discuss each of these questions separately. Question #1 is about the jerk who butts in front of you in line at the grocery store. The under-chutzy person moves out of the way, says nothing, and avoids eye contact. The chutzy, successful person gets in her face and deals with the problem directly. The over-chutzy person screams, yells, and makes a scene causing embarrassment for everyone. I bet, however, that jerk will think twice about butting in front of anyone in a store again.

Question #2 really happened to me. My son John and I were at the fast-food restaurant picking up donated napkins for a community-wide park clean-up day when I walked outside and observed a young man dropping a large drink carton out of his car window. I thought about (a) driving away and saying nothing. I also thought about (c). I really wanted to get in the car and ram him. But the creative chutzpah spirit overcame me. Instead, I went over to him, picked up the drink carton, and said, "Excuse me, but I think you dropped this. You look busy, so I will throw it away properly for you." I felt great. I was a role model. My son's jaw dropped to the ground as he observed the chutzy way I handled the situation. Chutzy people make great parents. They also make great companions. Read on.

Question #3 is a true scenario of a person in this book. The way Jimmy/Jay handled the situation has lessons for us all. The under-chutzy person becomes defensive and reacts childishly by avoiding further discussion. The over-chutzy person overreacts before getting all the facts. The successful, admirable person, however, bides his time, investigates the situation, then chooses an appropriate course of action. Jay's story shows how one young man handled this shocking and painful revelation and went on to become a successful judge.

In question #4, after such a tragedy, the under-chutzy person retreats, becomes fearful, and avoids contact with the world. The over-chutzy person becomes aggressive and remains in denial regarding certain changes. The successful, chutzy person not only faces her disability realistically, but gives back to others. She counts her blessings and shares her new insights. The story of Mary Ann and her struggles illustrates another inspiring approach to personal achievement.

Question #5 is about giving. The under-chutzy person under-utilizes his wealth. He gives to others, but modestly, quietly, and anonymously. The over-chutzy person doesn't give back at all. He lives only with selfish thoughts in an egocentric world. The truly successful, chutzy person remembers his roots and gives back to others. Eugene Lange created the "I Have a Dream Foundation" to share his wealth and improve the world. He gave in both monetary and personal ways. His story is an inspiration to us all.

Question #6 is very serious. Chutzy, successful people have dreams they continue to pursue no matter what obstacles or disappointments they encounter. Feel free to dream. Dare to dream. Dare to take risks. Chutzy people are successes because they listen to themselves and they persevere.

My research into what makes a person successful resulted in a description of 10+ traits shared by my heroes. Pick one, two, or all of them to help you overcome your obstacles to become more of the successful person you truly deserve to be.

3

Success

*"Success is to be measured not so much by the
position that one has reached in life, but by the
obstacles he has overcome while trying to succeed."*
—BOOKER T. WASHINGTON

I am wildly successful and want you to be also. I consider myself successful because I am learning who I am and how to take advantage of my uniqueness to achieve personal and professional goals. I do not have a lot of money, but I make the best use of what I have. I have overcome a number of obstacles in my life and know that there will be many more to come. I am successful because I welcome challenges and appreciate the opportunities I have to help others and to make the world a better place.

What is success to you? Success can mean many things, but involves the elements included in achieving one's needs and wants, whatever they are. Success is not a destination but a journey, a series of steps taken toward one's desired goals and outcomes. Webster defines success as: "A degree or measure of succeeding; a favorable or desired outcome; the attainment of wealth, favor, or eminence." Other affiliated terms include: to make progress, advance, get ahead, go places, find one's way, prosper, reap the fruits or benefit of, reap or gather the harvest, make one's fortune, turn to good account, win, prevail, triumph, gain mastery, win out, carry the day, have the best of it, have it all, have it all one's way, set the pace, have the world at one's feet, surmount or overcome a difficulty or obstacle, and make headway. Success, therefore, has many meanings, and must be defined by the individual seeking it. Success may be as simple as getting what you want in life and wanting what you get.

Your Needs

SOME NEEDS ARE CONSISTENT throughout the human race. Psychologist Abraham Maslow, in describing his "Hierarchy of Needs," theorized that people are motivated to satisfy needs. Needs have levels, but the basic biological needs must be met first. For example, an infant must be fed and nurtured in order to grow physically and psychologically. As the child grows, needs at a higher level serve as a motivating force. To achieve the ultimate experience of fulfilling one's potential and becoming self-actualized (the highest level of need), all the lower needs must be satisfied. These include the need for biologic integrity, the need for safety and security, the need for belonging in love, the need for self-esteem and ego satisfaction, and, ultimately, the need for self-actualization.

Another way to look at Maslow's hierarchy of needs is to describe them according to the following: physical, environmental, emotional, sociological, cultural, and spiritual. People need to succeed at each lower need level in order to proceed to the next. A person who does not have enough food or adequate shelter will hardly be in a position to work toward self-actualization. Likewise, one who lacks adequate love or self-esteem will be out-of-balance and will have to satisfy those needs before moving on to the ultimate level of success, that of personal achievement and self-actualization.

Self-actualization, the striving to reach one's fullest potential, is what success is all about. However, our notions of success are continually changing. In the United States, the concept of success has shifted dramatically over the lifetime of most of us who are adults. In the 1950's success meant having a family, a father with a job, a stay-at-home mother, and 2.3 healthy but not too rebellious children. In the 1960's success meant the elimination of some of these traditional roles, allowing men and women to fulfill themselves with alternative careers and lifestyles. In the 1970's we all worked and made a lot of money. In the 1980's we spent the money, and in the 1990's we are wondering if we will ever have money again! So the concept of success, particularly in regard to financial success, has been a changing notion over the last half century. How have your notions of success evolved since childhood?

What is not Success

WHILE WHAT IS SUCCESS may be individual, what is not success may be universal. Success is not doing things just to make others happy. It is not living the dreams of your parents, but living your own dreams. Success is not being too fearful to pursue dreams or even too closed-minded to have them. Success is not quitting or failing to make steps towards your dreams. Being too cautious to take risks is also not success, nor is being too focused, out-of-balance, selfish, self-absorbed, unimaginative, thankless, humorless, or self-destructive. Success is the opposite of these things.

Your Way

THREE MAJOR LEAGUE UMPIRES were at dinner discussing how they make their calls. Umpire Number One stated, "I call it as I see it!" Umpire Number Two said, "I call it as it is!" And Umpire Number Three topped them all: "It ain't nothing till I call it!"

Umpire Number Three had great chutzpah. He knew who he was and the importance of his impact on the world around him. And he wasn't afraid to say so. Success comes from living life your way and seeing the world as Umpire Number Three sees his call: "It ain't nothing till you call it!"

Chutzpah & Success

HAVING CHUTZPAH will give you the courage, confidence, and perseverence to face yourself and others, to dream your dreams, and to move forward despite obstacles. It will help you become more creative and change your personal view of things to suit you better. It will give you the gall and gumption to succeed, for success, in the words of Benjamin Disraeli..."is the child of audacity."

In order to be successful, we must face our fears, dream our dreams, take risks, find balance, give back, open our minds and our eyes, count our blessings, love ourselves, laugh at life, and be willing to start over again many times. How do I know these things? Because my friends have taught them to me. You will see in the stories that follow how my friends and heroes demonstrate these traits in the achievement of their own successes. You will also see that success means something different to each of them.

Marie's success comes from being able to face her abusive parents and choose a healthy life over a hurtful one. Mills Lane's success comes from the persistence to become a prize fighter, a nationally respected referee, and then a judge. Caryl's success is the accomplishment of her dream to own her own business. Dr. Snider's success comes from how he helps others dream. Bill is successful because he knows the kind of risks to take and those to avoid. Valerie is successful because she has found the necessary balance in her life to survive self-destruction. Eugene Lange and Ondra Berry, from opposite sides of the tracks, find success as mentors as they continue to give and give back.

Jay became successful when he learned not to walk in the shadow of his mother. Mary Ann is successful because she survived a devastating auto accident with resultant brain injury and has become a motivational speaker. Joe's success is from finding humor and passing it on to corporations. Tom's success comes from ignoring naysayers and approaching his challenges as frontiers, not limitations. And Alice is successful because she boldly started life over when she could have been retiring.

These are just some of the stories you will read which describe differing notions of success. I know you will find inspiration in them.

Part II

The 10+ Traits of Chutzy, Successful People

4

Trait #1

Face
Your Fears

*"Success comes to those who are neither afraid
to fail nor discouraged by failures."*

The first step in cultivating more chutzpah is to face your fears. Throughout history, the most common debilitating human ailment has been cold feet. Check your feet. Are they cold? Is there some dream you haven't pursued because of fear? How much courage does it take to not only accept the challenges that are facing us, but to embrace them and find a unique way to solve them?

We face a lot of fears. What is it that we are afraid of? What keeps you from doing the next thing or getting to your next level? Many of us are afraid of rejection. Others are afraid of failure. But let me ask you, how many of you have learned more from your failures than you have ever learned from your successes? It seems that the things we experience from our failures make deep impressions and we tend to learn from them. We spend time analyzing what went wrong to make sure we don't repeat our mistake. This analysis is important, for we can turn a failure into a learning experience if we ask two questions: 1) What were the lessons learned? and 2) What were the gifts received? If you can look at each failed endeavor as a lesson or a gift, then that experience cannot possibly be a failure. Once we stop fearing failure, then we can move forward to be successful.

As Art Mortell writes in his book *The Courage to Fail*, success is actually based on *failing* most of the time. Without adversity, there is no growth. Successful people, in fact, do what they fear most. We rarely fail or succeed completely. Within every success are some failures, and vice-versa. We mature and develop by facing our fears, then by asking what have we done right to get this far and what will get us further next time. Successful people learn from their failures and choose to recover quickly from them. After a failure or a loss, we need the courage to rebuild and create again. According to Mortell, there are only two ways to fail. One is to not try and the other is to quit. But many of us characterize fear of failure as discomfort, and mistakenly try to stay in a comfort zone that keeps us from reaching out, trying something new, and achieving our dreams. Comfort becomes boredom, which is anathema to success. Jack Lemmon is quoted as saying, "Fear of failure will absolutely destroy you. You walk down the middle of the street, you never take chances, you never go down the little side streets that you look at and say, 'That looks interesting, but I don't know that street. I'll stay right here and just walk this straight line.'"

So facing fears takes courage. It takes courage to move out of one's (dis)comfort zone, take risks, and seek a higher level of achievement and success. One of my favorite baseball quotes is, "Life is like being a pitcher. In order to get your strikes, you have to risk your balls."

Marie

IN ORDER TO MOVE FORWARD in life, it is vital to face those people or experiences that have kept you from achieving your goals. As Marie's story illustrates, one cannot be successful in life without confronting one's demons – whether real or imagined. In Marie's case, the demons were very real indeed. The level of success she currently enjoys in her life is due to her willingness to face those demons head-on and take some serious risks.

Marie's biggest achievement in life these days is that of being a wife and a mother. Now you may not think this is a particularly big accomplishment in a person's life, but for someone with Marie's background it certainly is. For you see, throughout most of Marie's life, she was abused by her father. As if being beaten and told she was stupid weren't bad enough, Marie's father began to sexually molest her when she was 12 years old. Marie didn't know it at the time, but her older sister had also gone through the same ordeal until she finally forced her father to stop by threatening to report him to the police.

Marie already felt stupid and inadequate, but the sexual abuse made her want to "fade into the walls." She thought her mother must have known of the sexual abuse. But if she did realize what was going on, Marie's mother did nothing, and the abuse continued. It once again took the threats of Marie's older sister for the assaults to cease.

Marie did not realize what a bright child she was, and apparently neither did anyone else. In her senior year of high school, her counselor told Marie that she was not college material and should probably consider secretarial school instead. But Marie was desperate to leave home, so she moved out and enrolled at the local university to study nursing. She switched majors after two years, got a teaching credential, and threw herself into her work as an instructor at a local business college.

Although Marie's career was progressing well, her personal life was not. She endured an eight-year abusive relationship with one man, then finally left him after six months of therapy. It wasn't until the last session that Marie told her therapist about her father, a story she had kept secret for 28 years. The therapist suggested group sessions with people who had the same abuse experiences, but Marie felt she couldn't face that. Marie thought she was "cured" and moved on to marry another man.

This first husband was an alcohol, drug, and sex addict who was almost as abusive to her as her father had been. She went along with most of his perversions, feeling progressively worse about herself as time went on. Marie was excelling in her professional life, but her personal life was in such a shambles that she considered suicide. Once again she had reached a point where she couldn't stand her life anymore, and in an attempt to quell her thoughts of suicide, Marie sought therapy and agreed to group sessions. With a great deal of help from the group and her friends, Marie soon left her first husband to start her life over – this time alone.

At her first meeting, she was shocked to discover that there were more than 100 people there who relayed stories which were similar to or worse than Marie's experiences. She further surprised herself when she opened her mouth and her story just tumbled out. No one in the group criticized her or looked down on her, as Marie had feared they would.

Getting the story out in the open was the first step in Marie's healing. For the next three years, she continued with her therapy groups. It took a long time, but Marie finally realized that what had happened to her was not her fault. While

Marie had reached a high level in her therapy and her cure, she still had one major hurdle to cross – that of confronting her parents. As part of her ongoing therapy, she had to tell them what they did to her was wrong, that it had caused her a great many problems throughout her life, and that things would have to change.

Marie was terrified. She had never confronted anyone before. With all the secrets she had harbored throughout her life, she had become very good at covering things up and making everything seem fine. Her therapist helped her write a number of different scripts on how to confront her mother and father, depending on how they reacted to the meeting. But she was still terrified.

When her parents unexpectedly came to town one day, Marie knew it was time to face them. She insisted that they come to her house. She seated them in the appropriate places, as she had rehearsed in her scripts, stood before them, and with great courage, determination – and chutzpah – Marie told her parents that the physical abuse had been horrible and inexcusable, and that it had affected her in a number of negative ways. Her parents didn't say a word. So Marie continued.

She then told her parents what she thought of the sexual abuse. Her mother sat stone-cold quiet and never uttered a word. Marie's father sputtered a bit and said he had never intended to hurt her and that he thought he was actually helping to "educate her about sex." Marie was appalled at his response but kept her cool.

The next part was actually the hardest. She told her mother and father that unless they admitted their wrongdoing and went into therapy, she would no longer be a part of their lives. She was adamant. Marie was being as charitable and loving as a daughter could be in those circumstances by giving them the opportunity to make amends and keep the family together. But her parents refused to admit that they had done anything wrong or that they needed any psychological help. They stood up, shook their heads, and walked out of her house. In doing so, they also walked out of Marie's life forever.

While Marie was relieved to have spoken her piece, she was also saddened by the ending of the relationship and how it would affect the rest of her family. Her sisters were still in denial, had not discussed the situation with others, and had continued to maintain a relationship with their parents. But Marie could not do that. She wanted more for herself and became the black sheep of the family. Marie had faced her fears by risking the confrontation with her parents and had both failed and succeeded at the same time. She failed to get what she needed from her family, but she was successful in moving on to a new level of emotional health. Her life would never be the same. New confidence grew in her from being able to face her parents, and Marie started to look at herself as a different young woman.

A few months later, Marie met Mark, a man who, despite learning all about her past, still fell in love with her. They became engaged, and married on St. Mathew's Day. After returning from their Hawaiian honeymoon, they began to discuss having children. With Marie's background, it was an issue that had to be addressed openly, and they both knew it would be a difficult decision either way.

When Marie became pregnant not long afterward, she was struck by many emotions: excitement, anticipation and – one which was directly related to her own history of abuse – fear. She worried whether she could protect a daughter from the terrible things that had happened to her. She thought that having a son would be easier, so when her sonogram results came back confirming that Marie was carrying a girl, she sat down and cried. Although she was very fearful, she knew that with the love and support of her friends and husband, she would be a good mother, Mark would be a terrific father, and their daughter would have a safe and wonderful life.

Matty was born on October 26, 1994, to two weary but delighted parents after 44 hours of induced labor and medical difficulties. It took Marie many months to heal from the physical trauma of the delivery, but every time she looks into the eyes of her daughter and her husband, she knows it was all worth the pain. You see, there are no more secrets for Marie. She is able to love her husband and her child openly and completely. And while she still feels sadness that she no longer has her own parents in her life, there is also relief and continual healing for Marie.

"You can't survive without chutzpah," Marie says. "You need to stand up to others and let them know they can't push you around. Except for my daughter Matty, of course."

My Fears

FEAR TAKES MANY FORMS, but the results are the same – inaction, disability, and mediocrity. It is impossible to be successful without identifying your fears and facing them head-on, as Marie did. I have had to remind myself of that many times, for I, too, know about fear firsthand.

In 1981, the last thing I wanted to do was face my fears. I was in a situation that I was not happy with, yet I knew I would have to make changes if I were to move forward with my life. I was divorced and had a two-year-old son. I worked for an insurance company, but felt I was going nowhere. At that point in my life, my biggest fear was to stay where I was.

So I took a big chance and enrolled in a master's degree program in speech communication. I wanted to learn more about the dynamics of medical communications. As the director of administration for a medical malpractice insurance company, my job was to train physicians and their staff to improve communications with patients. Graduate school was wonderful and exciting, and surpassed even my expectations. But it was not easy to have a full-time job, a small, sick child, and attend classes evenings and weekends. I saw my health deteriorate and my energy level subside to almost nothing. I became ill with hypoglycemia and found myself unable to sleep at night and unable to stay awake during the day. I would start to cry for no reason and was unable to stop. There wasn't a day I wasn't afraid – afraid of losing my health, afraid of being a bad mother, afraid of losing my job, and afraid of failing. After two years, I found it impossible to do everything, so I gave up graduate school. This was the first big risk I had taken in my life and career and, in a sense, I had failed at it. There is no way to explain how overwhelmingly disappointed I was, because this was the first time in my life that I had not finished something I had begun. But the story doesn't end there.

On April Fool's Day 1985, I started my own business, Professional Liability Consultants, Inc. The insurance company with whom I had worked for seven years gave me a contract to go out on my own as a consultant and provide liability risk management programs for them. They had opened the door for me to attract other clients and to grow my business in any direction I chose. It was a wonderful opportunity, but I was very afraid. Again, what if I failed? What if I could not honor the commitment to my first client, the insurance company? How much energy would I use up, time would I waste, and money would I lose if I were not successful at this new endeavor?

So my consulting contract with the insurance company was

just a start. To survive, more clients were needed. I undertook new projects and met new people. Every day, I forced myself to do something that scared me to death. I started developing communication training programs for other professionals to expand my client base. I rode around with police, health inspectors, building inspectors, and DMV testers in order to study the communication needs of these professionals and to create programs specific to them. I also reenrolled in graduate school.

It wasn't until this second attempt at graduate school that I discovered how much I enjoyed speaking to groups. Although I had never taken a public speaking or debate course, I found myself developing and presenting training programs. My instructors commented on my talent for speaking and for audience interaction, and encouraged me strongly to do more of it. I finished my Master's Degree in speech communication the day before my 39th birthday. (Not bad for a woman who took years to overcome a speech impediment she had as a child!) Now, I train professionals on a full-time basis, teach others how to speak and present themselves, and help prepare them for employment interviews, trial appearances, and other critical life encounters.

But none of this would have been possible if I had not faced my fears and taken many risks. To go back to school, to learn how to speak in front of a crowd, to start my own business, and to force myself to do something new – and scary – every day. If I can do it, you can do it.

The Energy of Fear

IN MY CAREER as a professional speaker, I have found many opportunities to help others address their fear of public speaking. Are you aware that fear of public speaking ranks second on the list of all-time fears? Fear of snakes is first. In fact, fear of death only ranks somewhere around sixth. Of course, my personal fear as a public speaker is *death* while *speaking*. Seriously, I have learned a lot about fear from working through my own and others' stage fright.

Helen Hayes put it very succinctly when she said, "It took me years to figure out what to do with that fear and stage fright. I call it the butterflies. It finally occurred to me that the goal was not to get rid of the butterflies, but to get them to *fly in formation*." As a trained and talented professional, she did not turn away from her fear or try to eliminate it completely. Instead, she put it to good use. She felt the fear and used it to energize her many magnificent performances. So must we all. Feel the fear, take its energy, and do it anyway.

Facing Fear

Successful people feel the fear and work right through it. In order to have more chutzpah, we all need to face our fears and ask the following questions:

1. **What are we truly afraid of?**

Fear of failure? Fear of success? Or perhaps a combination of failure and success?

Fear of failure can paralyze us, but failure is a learning tool for success. Successful people recount their failures as stepping stones to achievement.

Other people seem to fear success. They have been thinking of themselves as failures for so long, that they may only be comfortable in those miserable shoes. They do not feel worthy of success, and know that if they do allow themselves to succeed, their lives will be irrevocably changed. These people are more fearful of change than they are of their present situation. How sad it is to fear success.

2. What is the likelihood that what we fear will come to fruition?

Mark Twain said that he had many fears in his life, some of which actually came true. Most of what we fear does not happen. We spend a great deal of negative energy worrying about problems which do not occur. Why waste so much time fearing things which will not happen? It is a much better use of our energy to face our fears head-on, like Patty did, eliminate them from our thoughts, and move ourselves to our next level.

3. What is the worst possible thing that can happen and what is that likelihood?

This is a good exercise for the most logical of you. It is also an exercise used by therapists when helping patients face what they are really anxious and fearful about. Go ahead. Imagine the worst possible thing that could happen when considering your fear. Then ask yourself, what is the statistical likelihood that it will happen? A friend of mine, going to a therapist before her pending divorce, was very fearful of breaking up the marriage. "What do you fear most?" the kind therapist asked her. She was shaking and crying and tears were rolling down her cheeks. Many notions passed before her, but finally she blurted out, "I am afraid my husband will take the baby away from me." The therapist asked softly, "What is the true likelihood that he will do that?" She stopped sobbing for a moment and a little smile emerged on her lips. "Not very likely," she said. "This guy can't take care of himself, much less a sick, crying child. I can't even get him to feed the goldfish every morning. I really don't believe he will take the child away from me." Indeed, he did not. And the two of them came to an amicable agreement regarding the divorce and the visitation opportunities.

4. **What will happen if we do not work through the fear and stay where we are?**

This is, of course, where I found myself some years ago when I was still at the insurance company. At some point, the pain of the present situation overcomes the false sense of security we associate with it. Most of us wait until the pain of one option overcomes the pain of another before we face our fears and move forward. Why don't we face these fears a little sooner and, in fact, search them out aggressively. Fears are challenges to overcome. Mrs. Galbraith, the mother in *Cheaper by the Dozen,* says that she awakens every morning and asks her Creator what challenges will be ahead of her that day. She looks forward to them and to facing her fears, because she believes that is how she gets to her next level. We should all look at our fears as these kinds of challenges – opportunities to move forward and onward to our next levels of success.

"Fear is the noose that binds 'til it strangles,"
— Jean Toomer, Writer

It takes chutzpah to face our fears and work through them. Whether it be in facing a boss or coworker, making a job or life transition, getting married, getting divorced, going to school, climbing a mountain, or writing a book, fear is a good thing. It energizes us and mobilizes us to move forward. Stare down your fear, laugh in its face, and do the deed. Using the energy of our fears to accomplish our goals is great chutzpah. It is not our job to eliminate the butterflies, but, as Helen Hayes said, "to get them to fly in formation."

5

Trait #2

Be
Persistent

"Success comes in cans, failure comes in can'ts."

Studies of successful people consistently show that the number one trait they share is persistence – not intelligence, not luck, but the ability to just keep on going. Babe Ruth was persistent when he continued to pick up that baseball bat, even though he knew the odds were against him even getting on base. My son's Little League baseball coach, Coach Godfrey, frequently told the boys, "It's a fact, 87% of the time you can't hit the ball unless you swing the bat." That's a pretty accurate statistic – or maybe just a facetious way to tell the boys that in order to succeed, you have to try and try again.

Getting up one more time than you fall down takes persistence and is a key to success. Mills Lane, now a judge and nationally known boxing referee, knows all about falling down and getting back up. Growing up on a farm in the south, Mills' life had been mapped out for him by his strict, disciplinarian father. The plan was for Mills to finish high school, to study forestry and agriculture at college, and then return to the family farm.

Mills wasn't allowed many of his own thoughts or opinions, but he knew this was not the life for him. His father was against everything Mills wanted for himself. Mills also knew that he would have to stand up to his father and take charge of his own life, but he feared the wrath of the old man. However, Mills was persistent and a bit rebellious. For many years, most of what he accomplished was in direct contradiction to his father's wishes. His father was against him going into the Marine Corps after high school, but finally consented when a friend told the father it would be a good idea for this undisciplined, undirected young man. His father was against boxing, so Mills became a boxer. His father was against him becoming an attorney, so he enrolled in law school at the age of 30.

Mills had a great deal of chutzpah in standing up to his father and rebelling against his tyrannical rule. But chutzpah isn't just about rebellion. It is about standing up for oneself, standing up for others, and standing up for what's right. Although there were many things Mills rebelled against in his father's home, there were many good things he learned there also. He developed a strong sense of patriotism and values – values which serve him well in his position as a district court judge and as a referee for the World Boxing Association. Imagine a short, 150-pound man pushing in between two heavyweight boxers – the ultimate chutzpah. None of this success would have been possible without perseverance and determination. From his meager beginnings on the farm to his position as judge and referee, there have been many bumps along the road. Small in stature, but with a mean, lean, wiry build, Mills has seen his share of fights – in his personal life; in his relationship with his father; and in his professional life as a boxer, a referee, a district attorney, and a district court judge.

"In my first pro fight, I got knocked out in 38 seconds. It

was a good lesson, too, 'cause I had just got back from the Olympic trials and everybody told me I was the greatest thing that ever came to Reno. I was gonna set the town on fire. They put me in with this kid from prison, Arty Cox. He could punch, but he was a dog. And not a real good fighter. They told me I could eat this guy alive. I remember going down two times. I remember I went to the corner and they gave me ammonia. And so I looked up at my coach and said, Well, what happened?' and Coach says, It's all over.' And I said, You mean I knocked him out that quick?' And he says, 'Yeah, you really knocked him out.' So I learned the importance of persistence and working hard. I fought Cox again in Sacramento and knocked him out in the third round. But that first fight is the one I remember."

Mills uses this persistence to overcome his fears, as do other chutzy people. "Sure, I have fear. Whenever I climbed into the boxing ring, I'd be scared. If you weren't a little scared, you'd either be crazy or lying. I'm also scared of taking my robe off and not having any trunks on. That's what happened to a guy one time. He put his cup on, got taped, put on his robe, and just forgot his trunks. So I always check. You gotta have a little bit of fear. The butterflies are your friends. They help you do the best job you can."

Facing his fears and striving to new levels of success have taken dogged persistence. "I don't have great natural talent, but I have some tools, and I'm gonna make the best of them. If my opponent runs three miles, I'm gonna run four. If he works out in the gym two days, I'm gonna work out three days. If he hits the bag six rounds, I'm gonna hit eight. I'm gonna outwork him. Same thing about being a prosecutor. You show me an esoteric son-of-a-bitch, I'll beat him every day. I'll just outwork him. Those folks who sit on their asses because they have some natural intellect or some natural brain power, you can always outwork them. I don't have the brains that many other people have, but when I get into the ring, I tell my opponent, If you're gonna fight me, you're gonna fight me all night long."

Fighting the fight all night long is what persistence is all about. Other heroes have likewise used persistence in their own fights. Eleanor Roosevelt, a woman told by a relative she was too homely to ever wed, married her cousin. Without much formal education, she became one of our country's most outstanding first ladies – and walked with kings, queens, and other world leaders. Once, she even had a meeting with Kruschev. Afterwards he said, "That was an interesting lady. At least we didn't shoot each other." And she was persistent. After World War II she was told there was no way to help the 30 million homeless children in Europe, but she wouldn't take "no" for an answer. With the help of the United Nations, she founded UNICEF and helped many of those 30 million people. One day at a time, one step at a time, she persisted, never listening to naysayers.

Thomas Edison, who was kicked out of school for not being bright enough, lit the world with his invention of the light bulb. How much persistence did it take for him to discover thousands of ways that a light bulb could *not* be made? He never faltered nor doubted his pursuit. In fact, each time he failed to light up the bulb, he congratulated himself on finding yet another way that it would not work. What great chutzpah it took for Edison to keep trying in "light" of all those failures. Helen Keller, who could see no light, persisted in making herself a whole human being and inspired others who face limitations and disability. Abraham Lincoln's entire life is a tribute to persistence. Before becoming president and one of our greatest leaders, Lincoln failed many times in business, in politics, and in his personal life.

Persistence is the ability to keep on going, even in light of obstacles and adversity. It includes determination, tenacity, perseverance, and resilience, and is thereby, the very essence of chutzpah. Very little worthwhile in this world comes easily. Progress and success are the result of some sacrifice, as well as the courage to keep on going. It takes persistence to achieve your dreams and attain your goals. You must be persistent to lose weight, learn a sport, start a business, speak a new language, write a book, be a good parent, spouse, friend or coworker. It means overcoming procrastination, making a plan, and taking small steps in the right direction.

The persistence it takes to work toward one's goals has a two-pronged benefit. The first is the increased likelihood that the goal and success will be achieved. The second is the improved self-esteem you develop as you progress. Nothing feels worse than being a quitter, knowing that there were more things you could have done to attain your goals but that you stopped short for a number of self-limiting reasons. Conversely, nothing feels better than accomplishment. Success, indeed, fuels more success.

Why People Give Up

MOST OF US HAVE FEAR when attempting something new. Public speakers describe having the same fear – stagefright – that others have but persist in giving their presentations. Other people give up because of that fear. They worry that they are not good enough. If they give it their all and still fail, then their self-esteem will be seriously compromised.

Have you given up only because you are impatient and expect positive results more quickly? Today's society does not seem to recognize nor teach the value of delayed gratification, something our parents and forebearers had to learn. Without the sacrifice incumbent in delaying gratification, many people will give up due to sheer impatience. What a shame. "I tried that once, but it didn't work," is the excuse of the quitter. Perhaps "it" needs to be tried many more times and in different ways. The definition of neurosis is doing the same thing over and over again the same way and expecting a different outcome.

In order to be successful, then, we must be persistent in not only trying and trying again, but in trying and trying in other ways. We must be creative and flexible, and we must keep approaching our goals from different vantage points.

When to be Persistent

SUCCESS REQUIRES BEING PERSISTENT from the beginning of the project right on through to the end. Overcoming procrastination is the first step in persistence. At some point, the tension and fear involved in *not* starting overcomes the tension and fear involved in starting. At this point, the plan must be laid out and the first step taken. An ancient Chinese proverb says, "A journey of 1,000 miles starts with the first step." Every accomplishment starts with a first step. Climbers learning how to scale a mountain are not taught to look at the top, but just at the first step and then each small subsequent step. After the first step is taken, each subsequent step should be planned and proceeded with in a logical progression. If your dream is to start a business, then you must have a business plan and start with the basics of funding, location, and developing expertise.

In order to stay inspired and persistent throughout the project, you must congratulate yourself for each progressive step, as small as it might be, and to keep getting up if you fall down. If something isn't working, try something different. Get help if necessary. If you have reached a plateau in your business, perhaps you need an expert in banking, finance, production, marketing, sales, advertising, retailing, or management. Do not be afraid to ask for help from others. It is often through the eyes of an outside expert that we get a new view of our situation, which helps us continue on with new energy.

It is also vital to persevere as you near the end of your project or goal. Many people quit right before they finish something. How many students do you know who quit college in their last year? What a shame to waste such time and energy and to face the rest of your life without that important diploma. The same can be said of runners who collapse right before the end of a race. The difference between winners and quitters is that winners keep their eye on the end and persist doggedly through it. Martial arts experts train people how to break through blocks by increasing their vision to *beyond* the point of the end of the block. This is what we must all do. We must persist not just to the end of our goal, but all the way through it.

When to Give Up

THERE MAY BE some situations which cannot be resolved or goals which cannot be achieved. The time may come when the efforts made toward unattainable goals should cease and the efforts put toward different ones. For example, married couples want a warm, loving home life. But if the relationship has soured and every attempt to improve it fails, including the use of outside counselors and therapists, it may be time to stop and move in a different direction.

The timing is very personal, but at some point we must make the decision not to "throw good money after bad." In the gambling town where I live, good players soon learn not to pursue a bad bet any further. Once the bet becomes untenable, then one must stop and limit one's losses.

We must *not* be persistent with situations which are wrong, painful, mean, or hurtful – to ourselves or to others. And we must be realistic. If a man in a wheelchair will never regain the use of his legs, then his persistence in trying to walk may be ill-founded. It might be better for him to use his persistence to learn new skills for his hands, eyes, ears, mouth, fingers, and nose – to help him learn how better to speak, write, or use a computer.

How to be Persistent

1. **Take the first step.** Overcome procrastination and allow the anticipated pleasure of taking that first step motivate you. You will be amazed how energized you become just taking that first step and anticipating the possibility of attaining your goal.

2. **Take small steps.** "By the yard it's hard, by the inch it's a cinch." Keep taking small steps. Nobody will ever criticize you for small steps, as long as they are continuous and go in the proper direction.

3. **Congratulate yourself at every step.** Look back at where you started and tell yourself, "good work, good job," for every small accomplishment.

4. **If you fall down, get up.** If you keep falling down, try something else. Get help, if needed.

5. **Let success fuel you.** Revel in the pleasure you feel from making progress and seeing yourself grow. Sometimes the steps toward the goal are more important than the actual attainment of the goal.

6. **If you are stuck somewhere and are losing your energy and enthusiasm, try it a different way.** Be flexible, be creative, but don't give up.

7. **Visualize the outcome and feel the pleasure of success.** There are many books written by experts on visualization and psychocybernetics. They describe the importance of relaxation, visualization, and involving all the senses in the feeling of accomplishment and success. There have been a great number of successes attributed to visualization. Olympic downhill skiers are trained to visualize the course before they take off down the hill. Many prisoners of war who came back to live relatively normal lives describe how their use of mental imagery and visualization helped them through the most trying and torturous of times. A study by Dr. Maxwell Maltz describes how visualization can be used to improve basketball playing. The fascinating results of his research showed that training people to visualize shooting hoops actually improved their scoring ability as much as those who physically practiced shooting hoops. It is obvious that we are just learning the power of visualization and its power to help us achieve our goals.

8. **Act as if you are successful.** If you are writing your first book, act like an accomplished author. If you want to be a good parent, act as if you are a good parent. If you want to own a successful business, act like a successful businessperson. If you want to lose weight, act like a healthy thin person. The mind has an amazing ability to help you create the behaviors necessary to be consistent with your thoughts. Anthony Robbins, in his book *Unlimited Power,* describes his techniques for helping people relieve depression by making them act as if they are not depressed. Again, this is just the tip of the iceberg in regard to the power of our mind.

9. **Just do it.** Whatever it is you want to do and want to be,

just do it and be it. Look at your obstacles as opportunities and simply become that which you wish to become. So, even if it takes all night, fight your fight and dream your dream.

If you still don't believe in your own power to achieve your goals through persistence – and if you are still making excuses that you are not talented, intelligent, educated, or lucky enough – then reflect on this quote from Calvin Coolidge...

"Nothing in the world can take the place of persistence. Talent will not; nothing is more common than unsuccessful men with talent. Genius will not; unrewarded genius is almost a proverb. Education alone will not; the world is full of educated derelicts. Persistence and determination alone are omnipotent."

"When things go wrong, as they sometimes will,
When the road you're trudging seems all uphill,
When funds are low and debts are high,
You want to smile, but you have to sigh.
When care is pressing you down a bit,
Rest if you must, but don't you quit.
Success is failure turned inside out,
The silver tint of the clouds of doubt.
And you never can tell how close you are,
It may be near when it seems afar.
So stick to the fight when you're hardest hit.
It's when things go wrong that you must not quit."

– AUTHOR UNKNOWN

6

Trait #3

Dare
to Dream

"Excellent day for dusting. Start with a few old dreams." – CHINESE FORTUNE COOKIE

In order to have more chutzpah, you must dare to dream. A dream is a vision of what could be. It is a hope and a projection for the future. In order to be successful, we must all dream about our next levels of success and then find ways to make our dreams come true. If we have no dream, we have no purpose, and without purpose our lives have no true meaning.

So what are your dreams? Do you dream of owning a beautiful home, completing your education, inventing a useful product, traveling the world, creating world peace, retiring early, having a spouse and family, winning a beauty contest, writing a book, or owning your own business? My friend Caryl had a lifelong dream to own her own business. But for the most part of her life, it appeared to be an unreachable dream.

Caryl

AS THE ONLY DAUGHTER born into a traditional patriarchal Italian family, Caryl was never encouraged to do anything except be a good Catholic wife and mother. The boys were encouraged to go into business, but certainly not the girls.

She helped out in her parents' restaurant for many years and loved the idea of owning a business and being independent. But Caryl lacked confidence, encouragement, and finances, so when her father died, her dream of owning her own business seemed only like a pipe dream, as her mother barely had the resources to support her and her brother.

Caryl married early and had three daughters by the age of 22. She should have been satisfied with this traditional life, according to the way she was reared, but she was not. To make things worse, when the girls were infants, Caryl's husband left, making it necessary for Caryl to work full time just to support the three little girls. Striving to overcome dissatisfaction had to be put on indeterminate hold while Caryl struggled for her family's survival.

But Caryl wanted more for them than just a life of survival. Deciding that an education was a priority, she attended college at night and worked during the day. She says her dream was so clear that the exhaustion hardly mattered. Most mornings she arose at 3:00 a.m., while it was quiet, to study. Sleep may have eluded her, but never her dreams. Every waking moment was dedicated to pursuing her education and a fuller life for herself and her daughters.

After completing her studies, Caryl worked in the non-profit sector for fifteen years and then went to work in the private sector for a special events company. The jobs were exciting and creative, but along the way she encountered some mean-spirited, inconsiderate, and critical people – too much for sensitive Caryl to handle. She had such trouble in these situations that she sought therapy to learn how to cope. The therapy benefitted her in many ways, helping her to face her fears of insecurity and teaching her to be more assertive. With a new sense of confidence, Caryl remarried. Rod, a business management consultant, enjoyed the results of Caryl's therapy and helped her renew her life's dreams.

Caryl had become more relaxed, more confident, and more able to ask for what she wanted in life, so when the owner of the special events company decided to close it down, Caryl made an offer to buy it. With tremendous fear mixed, of course, with excitement, determination, and a great bit of chutzpah, Caryl presented a proposal to buy the company. She was delighted when it was accepted and told Rod, "Honey, I can do this!"

Well, the words came out of her mouth easily, but the fear of failure persisted. Caryl was afraid she would not be able to rise to the occasion and that she would fail. Her inner voice mocked her, "You are not creative enough to plan these events. You're the detail person. You're much too practical and survival-oriented to take the risky steps necessary to make this company grow and prosper." But she worked through those nagging words and after the success of her first big event, she could finally say out loud, "Yes, I am creative!"

> *"Some men succeed because they are destined to,*
> *but most because they are determined to."*

Today, Caryl is a young, beautiful, chutzy businesswoman whose special events company is thriving. Caryl's job is to help others make their dreams come true also, even if just for an evening. She has just moved into a larger office, feels good about herself, and gives to others in many ways, for Caryl has found out that it is never too late to bloom and to achieve one's dreams.

Shattered Dreams

Del Snider had a "Great American Dream" also. He was going to become an astronaut. After attending Notre Dame and the U.S. Naval Academy, he was commissioned in the U.S. Air Force and planned to go to flight school when he turned 27. He was just 23 years old, however, when he enrolled in graduate school as an Air Force officer to study electrical engineering and computer design. He soon met a beautiful young woman, Calisse, a registered nurse, and they were married in February of 1958. In December of that year, Calisse informed Del that she was pregnant and that she also had a fatal kidney ailment. Around their first anniversary, Calisse gave birth prematurely to a son, Delmar, III, who died within four days. Six months later Calisse also died, after spending eight of her last twelve months in the hospital. Another tragic event was the loss of Del's brother, who, at 22, was killed in an auto accident in March of that same year. Del was still only 23 years old and went into shock.

Del was a strong, logical, intelligent young man, but he had an emotional side full of caring and sensitivity. His dream to become an astronaut was shattered. He no longer felt the need to reach the moon and the stars, but a new dream grew within him.

Through the ordeal in the hospital with his wife and newborn child, Del closely observed the role of medicine and, more particularly, the role of the physician in helping people through their toughest life times. So Del buried his emotions along with his wife, his son, and his brother, resigned from the Air Force, and enrolled in medical school.

He was good with computers, monitors, and chemicals, so with his great intellect and technical ability, Del chose anesthesiology for his specialty. But this was not enough for Del. His new dream was to combine the complex technology of anesthesiology with the opportunity to provide love and attention to patients to help them through a frightening time in their lives. For Del knows about fear and he knows about dark moments. In an attempt to fight off his depression, Del has become amazingly in tuned to the emotions of his patients.

Del has learned how to give people permission to feel and express themselves. He incorporates hypnosis to help his patients relax, and gives them suggestions and commands to help them survive their surgery and heal more quickly. Del loves to work with children. He sets his bulky frame on the bed right next to the child, holds her hand, and tells her it is okay to be afraid, that most people are afraid, and if she wants to cry, then that's okay, too.

"Sweet dreams," is what he says to his patients before he puts them under, and he does everything he can to make sure that they are safe and comfortable.

Sweet Dreams

THE SHATTERING OF Del's first DREAM resulted in a life he never would have anticipated. He never thought he would be a physician, and he says he feels privileged to have people trust him enough to put them to sleep and to care for them throughout surgery.

Many of us have had our dreams shattered. It takes great chutzpah to dream again. We must allow ourselves to grieve for the old dream, but then to move on. There is no limit to the dreams we can have. Perhaps Del never made it to the moon or the stars, but he does bring sunshine into the lives of all of his patients.

Why Dream?

"YOU GOTTA HAVE A DREAM. If you don't have a dream, how you gonna have a dream come true?" So sang Dirty Mary in *South Pacific*. Why dream? We dream for many reasons. As complex organisms, our minds never stop. As the only animal with the ability to remember the past and project into the future, we have a unique opportunity to structure our own lives. We dream at night and we dream during the day, and sometimes our night dreams guide us in the formation of our day dreams. Our unconscious mind knows many things and, given the opportunity, will guide us to success.

"Open up your mind and let your fantasies unwind" is a line in *The Music of the Night,* from *The Phantom of the Opera.* This beautiful song suggests that we relax our conscious mind and let our unconscious mind create fantasies for our lives and our futures. Sometimes we work and struggle so hard that we don't allow our fantasies to unwind. We stay in a practical, day-to-day survival mode, not unlike what Caryl felt about her style of life before her dream came true.

But our dreams stay with us. It is important to find ways to get in touch with them and put into motion the behaviors which will help us achieve them. You deserve your dreams and to have them come true.

Great Dreamers

THE WORLD HAS MOVED forward because of great dreamers. Henry Ford dreamed of motorized vehicles and the world of transportation has never been the same. Ghandi dreamed of world peace. Thomas Edison dreamed of illuminating the world. Albert Einstein dreamed of things beyond this world. King Arthur dreamed of a new world, Camelot, and so did

John Fitzgerald Kennedy. Thomas Jefferson, one of the founding fathers of this country, dreamed of a world based on equality and said, "I like the dreams of the future better than the history of the past." And Martin Luther King, Jr., mesmerized the world with his dream for a better future for all of us. "I have a dream that in the world to come a man will be judged by the character of his soul instead of the color of his skin."

There are, of course, big dreamers and there are smaller dreamers. The heroes mentioned above had big dreams and made big differences in the lives of us all. Many of our dreams are not as earth-shattering, but are as important nonetheless.

When I lived on a kibbutz in Israel after graduating from college, I was shocked to learn who the kibbutzniks really were. Although some were native Israeli *sabras,* many on this kibbutz were refugees from the Nazi holocaust in Europe. These survivors had every dream of their youth crushed by the events that took place during World War II in Europe. One would think that these people could no longer dream. But this was not the case. These kubbutzniks dreamed of a land where they could be safe, where they could rear children free of domination and destruction, where they could live their lives more fully. I remember one man who drove the tractor in the orchard of the kibbutz, a menial, laborious job, but one which was very important to him. This man was a refugee from Europe. An educated, accomplished scholar, he spoke five languages and had descended from a family of professionals. Today, he was happy to drive the tractor because it helped fulfill his dream of a better future for himself and for the other refugees. He and the other survivors dared to dream – and a bold dream it was.

What great chutzpah they showed in starting their lives over and building a better world for generations to come. What chutzpah it took for them to finally achieve their "field of dreams" – through their grief, their pain, and their loss.

Field of Dreams

THE MOVIE, *Field of Dreams*, appeared to be about baseball, but was really a story about second chances to fulfill one's dreams. The characters all had unfulfilled dreams and had wondered throughout their lives how things might have been different. Do you harbor unfulfilled dreams also?

"Build it and they will come" was the instruction given to Kevin Costner in the movie. He thought that meant to build a ballfield, and the fans and players would come. He was partially correct, but the metaphor involved in the title means something much broader. To me, it means that if you build your foundation, large and sturdy, and illuminate it brightly, your dreams will come true. How many of us have the second chance to make our dreams come true that was afforded to these characters?

This fictional representation of the importance of dreams gives us an important message. Build your foundation, dream your dreams, and go after them *now*. You may not have a second chance to rebuild a relationship with a family member. Or to become a ball player. Or to write a book. Or to start a business. Or to create world peace. Start today.

7

Trait #4

Take
Risks

"Success is only a matter of luck—
ask any failure."

"**W**hat is a nice boy like you doing in a place like this?" I asked my friend Bill. "You were brought up in a working class home near Boston, Massachusetts, graduated with a business degree from a Jesuit university, are married, have three small children, play golf seriously twice a week, and appear much too clean-cut to own and manage a casino." Bill laughed and settled back into his plush chair. "Life is a gamble," he said.

Life certainly is a gamble, but one would think there are enough risks in life without adding the uncertainties of casino gaming. Bill did not need to take the risks he has in order to achieve his successes in life. He was reared and educated to go into corporate America, encompass traditional values, and make his way into a more conventional environment. But after college, on his way to California to look for a career in some traditional profession like banking or finance, he made a pit stop in Nevada. On a whim, he started working as a blackjack dealer on the graveyard shift in a small, family-owned casino.

He loved to gamble, study odds, and partake of the action. Bill could have gone anywhere, but he was intrigued by gaming and by the human psychology of betting.

In his seven years on graveyard shift, he observed a great deal about human nature and became fascinated by the intricacies. His supervisors were impressed with Bill's interest in the industry, his agile mind, and his solid work ethic. He moved up quickly through the gaming ranks and, by age 29, was the club's general manager. This meteoric rise to management was unheard of within the gaming industry, which traditionally nurtured and promoted only those with long histories in, and close ties to, casinos.

Bill gambled that this was an industry he could influence. His personal mission was to make gaming more businesslike, and he fought many battles along the way. Many times he "went for broke" trying to change certain long-held policies and directions—changes needed for the good of the business, the employees, and all involved. In each of these circumstances, he risked his entire career in order to get his way. He knew he was taking chances, he knew he was gambling, but it felt right to take the risks. He convinced the owners to have regular board meetings and to start making decisions from a sound business perspective. Standing up to family business members took a great deal of courage and chutzpah. He knew he could get his marching papers at any time, but deep down he was confident that what he wanted was good for everyone, so he chose to take the risks.

And his risks have paid off. The casino is extremely successful and has remained highly competitive within an ever-fluctuating industry. Bill himself feels very successful. He has been able to combine his professional life, in a highly volatile business arena amid all its temptations and party atmosphere, with a warm, nurturing home environment.

"You have to take risks in this world to succeed," says Bill, "but never with your family or with your integrity. You must know who you are, risk only what you can, but never more than you can afford to lose. It's the same with gambling."

Taking Risks

WITHOUT TAKING RISKS, we will never attain all that we can and have our dreams come true. We read of the risks Marie took to confront her parents, how Caryl risked to start her business, and how Mills Lane risked every time he climbed into the boxing ring. Each made a calculated risk and each succeeded. We can all learn something about risk-taking from their stories.

To clarify, risk-taking is not about living dangerously. It's not diving into an empty swimming pool, jumping out of a plane without a parachute (or even with one, for some of us!), or driving down a dark road without any headlights. It is driving down a new road, a road you've never traveled before. Risk-taking is part of life; it's how we learn, how we love, and how we grow. It is daring to be yourself, to find yourself, to trust yourself. It's to experience life to its fullest.

In a later chapter on humor (Chapter 11), I relate the life of Norman Cousins and how he used humor to cure a debilitating disease. His is also a story about risk-taking. You will read that in order to survive, he took risks fighting traditional medicine in ways that he thought were necessary to save his life. Having triumphed over the disease, he took other risks that forced traditional medicine to rethink its approach to health and healing which have benefitted us all.

Taking risks is scary. Many human beings avoid risks in order to find or maintain security. Ironically, though, security does not exist; it is only an illusion. Helen Keller said, "Security is mostly a superstition. It does not exist in nature, nor do the children of man as a whole experience it. Avoiding danger is no safer in the long run than outrageous exposure...Life is either a daring adventure or nothing." And this wisdom is shared by a woman who thanked God for her handicaps, for it is through them that she found herself, her work, and her God.

The only real security we have is in our ability to change, to adapt, and to take chances to improve our lives and the lives of others. My grandparents, who had what I call the "immigrant gene," took great risks when they left their homes, immigrated to a new country, learned a new language, and developed new skills so life could be better for them and their children. For them, risk-taking wasn't an option. Neither is it for us; it is a necessity. So the decision is not *if* to risk, but *which* risk to take and *when*.

Many people resist risking for fear they will fail, but most of us learn more from our failures than from our successes. You learn about yourself, you face your strengths, your weaknesses, and your fears. That's what risk-taking is all about. It's the cowboy who gets back on his horse and the Olympic diver who gets back on that springboard. Often the way to your brightest success is illuminated by your darkest failure.

How many of us worry about things which never come to pass? And how much of our good, positive energy are we wasting? When we let the fear of risking paralyze us, we are unable to move forward. In the words of Franklin Delano Roosevelt, "Let me assert my firm belief that the only thing we have to fear is fear itself. Nameless, unreasoning, unjustified terror which paralyzes needed efforts to convert retreat into advance."

Our greatest fear should not be what we might lose by risking, but what we will lose by *failing* to risk. Risks must be taken because the greater hazard in life is to risk nothing.

If you succeed in taking your risk, you've changed an important part of your life, perhaps forever; and change, to many of us, is unsettling. We don't take risks because we fear losing the so-called security of where we are. So we stay where we are and the risks and the years and our dreams pass us by.

Whether personally or professionally, it's true that risk takers face constant change. But *constant change is here to stay!* Change is not just a part of risk-taking, it is a natural part of life. If you never change, then you never grow, you never learn, and you never reach your goals. Booker T. Washington said, "Success is to be measured not so much by the position that one has reached in life as by the obstacles he has overcome while trying to succeed."

It is only when we explore our limits that we know our capabilities. That is the knowledge given by risk-taking. We also risk to love. It is only when we give ourself, risk ourself, and lose ourself that we can truly find love. According to Alfred Lord Tennyson, "'Tis better to have loved and lost than never to have loved at all." We also risk for others, to make their lives better. Christa McAuliffe did not venture into space just for Christa McAuliffe. She went into space for the children—our children. She risked and lost her life because she believed in teaching. She believed in bringing as much knowledge and experience into the classroom as possible, and her dream did not die when the space shuttle Challenger exploded. Today, a bit of her dream lives within us all.

We risk to win. Businesses do not succeed by caution. Businesses succeed by taking risks—by introducing new products, by retraining workers, and by rethinking their entire range and focus. And so do people. We risk our hearts to win love, we risk time and money to get an education, and we risk possible failure by daring to be ourselves, to try new careers, to move to a new town, to give a speech. We risk to make our dreams reality. To reach and reach out for our potential, we must all dream the impossible dream, for it may not be impossible at all.

I took risks to change my life for the better. I risked going back to school, learning to speak in front of a crowd, starting my own business, and forcing myself to do something new—and scary—every day. I do not want to consider what my life would be like now if I had not faced my fears and had not taken those risks. So let me now share with you a systematic approach to risk-taking, one which will help you achieve your field of dreams.

A Risk-Taking System

TO QUOTE YOGI BERRA, "When you come to a fork in the road, take it." The following are four distinct steps to help you take the right fork in the road.

Step #1 - Specifically define the risk you are going to take. Know what you are leaping into and why. Ask yourself, "Where do my passions lie? What are my dreams? What would I do even if I weren't paid to do it? Start a business? Get married? Sing in public? Run for office? Climb a mountain? Write a book?" You can turn your yearnings into earnings by being true to yourself and to your unique talents and by going in your own direction. List the pluses and minuses of the risk, and give a value to each according to how it matches your personal purpose and your life goals. Do you value independence or service to others or lots of money? Define your risk *exactly.* Dr. Tom Kubistant, author of *Performing Your Best* stresses that goals need to be both appropriate and attainable. He says that goals can be achieved in steps, so the process is as important as the end result. Know your values. In 1985, my values included the need for new challenges, independence, and more time with my child. Roy Disney, nephew of Walt, tells us that when our values are clear, decisions are easy. So is risk-taking.

Step #2 - Develop a risk plan. Spell out the steps involved in reaching your goal and develop a contingency plan for failure. Know what you will do if you don't succeed. Weigh the risks of doing *A* versus the risks of doing *B* versus the risks of doing nothing at all. Chart a course for yourself, but be willing to make mid-course corrections as necessary. Look forward to the journey, for the journey may really be your destination. Look at Columbus. He planned for India, but ended up in the Americas! And the world was never the same. Again, in my case, I decided if my business didn't work out, I could get another job in the insurance industry. Hopefully your contingency plan won't be as drastic as Lee Iacocca's, who said that if the government didn't guarantee Chrysler's needed loans, his plan B was to close up shop and put thousands of people out of work!

Step #3 - Check for timing. Risks, like everything else, require that you act only when the time is right. What's going on in the world? Are conditions optimal? Guess what? They never will be. Don't get a case of "analysis paralysis." The timing is always a guess. Don't rush, but don't delay. Risk when the odds are at your best and watch for signs. Nobody can tell you exactly what the signs will be, so you need to be on the lookout for them.

There is a Zen saying, "When the student is ready, the teacher appears." This has certainly been true for me. Shortly before I started my business in April of 1985, I had lunch with Dr. Del Snider, the anesthesiologist from Chapter 6, "Dare to

Dream." He casually asked how I was doing. I said, "fine," but obviously my body language indicated otherwise. "Idora, I ask you again, how are you doing?" he probed further in that hypnotic, persuasive tone.

I looked into his soft blue eyes, knew he was a man I could trust, and blurted it out. "I am terrified. I'm starting this new business next month and I don't know if it's a good idea. I am giving up a secure position with the insurance company to do God-knows-what. I don't think I can do anything but underwrite malpractice insurance and can't imagine how I can possibly make a living. Am I making a big mistake?"

Dr. Snider took his time to reply. "Idora," he said, "you will learn many new things about yourself when you are out on your own. You will find that many of the functions you handled at the insurance company will translate themselves into ways to earn your living. Your fear is natural and your doubts are normal, but don't let them hold you back. When you return to the office today, make a list of every job you perform for the insurance company and imagine how each can be turned into a service for other clients. Then take two aspirin and call me in the morning," he added with a chuckle.

I looked at him and felt my mouth drop open. I had never thought of my services in that way before. Through the reflection in his eyes, I saw myself as the successful businesswoman I would become. Whether he knew it or not, he had become my mentor. I must have been ready. It was obviously the right move and the right time.

Step #4 - Take the risk. This is it. This is where you move. This is where you take everything you've learned and apply it. Keep your goals in mind and focus on them. Develop new habits to pursue those new goals. Obstacles are what you see when you lose sight of your goals, so don't turn back. Aim high and be persistent. Remember the story of the youthful-looking man who was arrested for selling fountain-of-youth pills he claimed would reverse the aging process. The judge asked if there was a record for prior arrests. "Yes, Your Honor," said the city attorney. "He was arrested in 1979, 1963, 1950, 1938, 1903, 1887, and 1844." You must commit totally to your mission, stay focused, and don't give up.

Dr. David Viscott, who wrote *Risking,* gives us some final risk paradoxes. "Do your best," he says, "but don't argue with reality. Thank others for your successes, but don't blame them for your failures. Don't give up too soon, but don't hold on forever." As we say here in Reno, don't throw good money after bad. Be ready to cut your losses if it becomes clear and prudent to do so. Trust that things will work out, but don't trust blindly. Take your own risks, but don't take other people's. Never risk your life unless the odds are with you; there is no such thing as a safe risk.

If, after all this planning, you are still unsure and afraid to leap, I want you to think about something. Don't think about all the risks you have taken, think about the ones you haven't. Think about the risks other people took, the ones that really belonged to you. It's time to look at yourself in the mirror and realize that the choice *not* to risk is just as critical and consequential a choice as the choice *to* risk. Every opportunity ignored is an opportunity lost; an opportunity that may never come again. As Ralph Waldo Emerson said, "All life is an experiment. The more experiments you make, the better." Let me add that the more at-bats, the greater the chance of home runs.

So what are you waiting for? Seize the moment. With every risk comes the chance to fulfill your dreams, to reach your potential, and to live a life that exceeds mere years in its spirit, fulfillment, and adventure. That's what risk-taking is all about. It's taking the steps necessary to live your life your way. So take that risk. Warm up those cold feet, start that business, climb that mountain, write that book, and keep on risking.

> *"Look to this day for yesterday is but a dream*
> *and tomorrow is only a vision. But today*
> *well-lived makes every yesterday a dream of*
> *happiness and every tomorrow a vision of hope."*
>
> —SANSKRIT QUOTE

Trait #5:

Find
Balance

*"The ladder of success must be set upon
something solid before you start to climb."*

We live in an oxymoronic world. It is a
world of conflict, contrast and opposites. We live in a world of
*jumbo shrimp, guest hosts, solemn jests, small disasters, final
approaches* and *fried ice cream.* Oxymoronic phrases by definition contain two words with opposite meanings paired
together to form a single phrase. We use these terms every day
and rarely recognize their contradictory nature. In such a world
of contradictions, it's no wonder that we have trouble finding
balance in our lives.

Being out of balance not only hurts us physically, emotionally and psychologically, but it can also keep us from being
truly successful. When we slip out of balance, the entire organ-
ism that comprises our body and mind feels stressed. Of
course, some stress is good for us, particularly the kind that
comes from trying something new, exciting and challenging, or
the kind that forces us to get moving on a project or goal. But
there is also bad stress – that which comes from our being out
of balance, out of homeostasis or equilibrium. In some cases,

this homeostatic imbalance makes it difficult to handle life's challenges and less possible for us to achieve the kinds of success to which we aspire.

Valerie

A GOOD EXAMPLE of how this organic imbalance can be dangerous is illustrated by the story of my friend Valerie. Valerie was born into the "ideal" American family.

Her father was a well-known attorney who loved his family and worked long, hard hours to provide financial security for them. Valerie's mother stayed at home to rear the children and provide support for the entire family. One sad day, however, Valerie learned that her all-American family was in jeopardy, as her father had fallen in love with someone else. Divorce followed.

Valerie loved both of her parents. She received a great deal of attention and affection from her mother, but she idealized the relationship with her father, who had been absent from much of her life. He was so charming, sweet and generous that she would do anything for his love and affection. It became very difficult for her when, after the divorce, she moved with her mother to another state. With her father living so far away, it was then even harder for Valerie to receive his love. So she left her mother's home and moved in with her father, her new stepmother, and step-siblings. It was a miserable life. Her stepmother felt threatened by Valerie, and the other children were cruel to her.

In an attempt to win her father's affection, attention and approval, Valerie became involved in a number of extracurricular activities. In addition to being an overachiever and award-winner at school, she served as an officer in several clubs and groups, became a Girl's Nation delegate, candy striper, and

Junior Citizen of the Year for her county. She even hosted a weekly talk radio program at a local radio station. But no matter how hard she worked and how many awards she garnered, her father remained distant and aloof.

Valerie continued to try to impress him. She graduated college in the top ten percent of her class and completed two master's degrees, one in journalism and one in contemporary literature. (She enjoys having M.A., M.A. after her name.) Still, she felt that her achievements fell short. Even the admiration of her husband, whom she married after completing her first M.A., was not enough to satisfy her. She decided she had to do more. So she and her husband agreed that she should pursue her dream to go to law school, which required Valerie to move miles away from her home and husband to attend classes.

Enrollees at this law school were all considered "C" students until they proved themselves otherwise. Valerie had never in her life been anything but an "A" student, but no matter how hard she worked, she could not reach that level. In her second year, she began attending an exercise class and went on a low-carbohydrate, low-calorie diet, hoping to lose a few pounds. While she lost weight, she gained a feeling of ultimate control. She reduced her food intake to 230 calories a day and became obsessed with losing weight. Even today, she remembers the exact diet she was on. For breakfast she ate two egg whites and sweetener; for lunch, one cup of lettuce with an inch of carrot and one-sixth of a pepper; and for dinner, one ounce of light cheese with one-half ounce of soy nuts. She refused to drink much water because it made her feel full. She stayed on this diet for six or seven months, dropping her weight from 137 pounds to 97 pounds, and then ultimately to 85 pounds. Valerie had become an anorexic.

Valerie remained actively anorexic for five years and knows all too well that she could have died. She became addicted to laxatives, diuretics, and appetite control pills. She obsessed about food but would not allow herself to eat it. She refused to socialize with people or attend any events that involved food. She withdrew from her friends and her family. As she became thinner and thinner, Valerie found herself wanting to withdraw from the world all together.

Anorexia has many physical effects. It weakens most of the body's systems, making it vulnerable to illness and injury. Valerie should not have been surprised, then, when she woke up one morning and could not move the right side of her body. In her sleep, she had rolled the wrong way onto her right shoulder and had severely injured her arm. The pain was so intense she could not lift her arm to brush her hair, open a car door, or even use a pencil. She continued to attend her law classes every day, but near the finals in her third year she was not physically able to write the exam and was forced to quit law school. It was the first time in her life she had quit anything. But her positive spirit persisted. "When I left law school, I left with my head held high, no money, no marriage, no health and no health insurance, but I was ready for something wonderful to happen."

Recovery from her injured arm took almost a year. Valerie moved back to her home city, lived by herself, and developed a personal philosophy to "simplify and resolve." She began to focus on the single most important thing in her life at that time – her health. As sick as she was, both physically and emotionally, she refused to succumb to a feeling of defeat. "We all serve as architects of our own lives," she says. "Why quit on a masterpiece?"

Day by day, bit by bit, and step by step, Valerie is healing herself. Through a great deal of introspection and positive self-analysis, she is achieving something she never thought important before – a sense of balance in her life. With a strong spiritual connection to religion, a positive attitude, a great sense of humor, and a willingness to share with others, Valerie is starting the next inning of her life with health and balance.

Her new approach to life was put to the test in 1988 when she had back surgery; a disk in her lumbar region was partially removed and a steel plate was implanted. She had to learn to walk again. At that time, her doctors told her that it would take her at least a year to recover and she might never be able to walk very well. With great poise, dignity, and chutzpah, she told her physician, "With all due respect, doctor, my belief in myself is more important than your medical opinion of me." She dove into physical therapy with the same commitment and fortitude with which she had faced other challenges in her life.

Valerie Finds Balance

TODAY, VALERIE IS MOST PROUD of three accomplishments. She considers her primary accomplishment the publication of her book, *Power Communications: Positioning Yourself for High Visibility.* After she had completed writing the manuscript, Valerie slipped it into a drawer, where it sat for a year. She wasn't sure it was "good enough" for anyone to publish. Finally, however, Valerie mustered the chutzpah to send it out. It was promptly published, and recognized by both Fortune Book Club and Money Book Club.

Valerie's second accomplishment involves her recovery from both her arm injury and her back surgery – in record time. She especially remembers the sense of achievement in learning how to walk again, well ahead of schedule.

Her third – and most enduring – accomplishment is her

newfound sense of balance. "It's not the 85 state and national awards I have won over the years that make me feel successful. Real success has flourished in my life since I discovered balance…that magical blend of relationships with family, friends, career, community, and church. Of course, I am still a work in progress."

Food and physical appearance still remain a challenge for Valerie. On any given day, she can recite exactly what she ate and how much she exercised. Fortunately, though, she can now live more comfortably with herself and with her body. Although she has no children of her own, and probably couldn't because of the many physical problems caused by anorexia nervosa, Valerie has stepped in as one of the world's greatest aunts to her nieces and nephews. She also donates time, love and money each year to the children who attend the elementary school built and named in honor of her father.

"By surviving self-destruction, I learned the importance of balance in my life," Valerie says. "Now I consider it my mission to give to others…to help children establish good, healthy self-esteem. This commitment requires that I first take especially good care of myself." Valerie takes good care of others, too. She is a wonderful, loving, supportive friend, and I admire her for her struggles, her determination, and her positive nature.

Living with Oxys and Other Morons

AS VALERIE'S STORY ILLUSTRATES, it takes great chutzpah to live with *oxy's* and other *morons* in today's world of opposites. In addition to the humorous oxymorons mentioned earlier, there are other seemingly contradictory notions of a more serious nature between which we need to find balance in order to succeed. These oxymorons include the need for *focus* and *flexibility, confidence* and *humility, honesty* and *hope,* and *patience* and *persistence.*

Focus and flexibility – In order to be successful we must find balance between focus and flexibility. We need to have both focused flexibility and flexible focus. First let's talk about focus. To reach our goals, we must remain focused; focus is power. It gives us the single-minded determination to reach a goal and not be deterred. It is to be so focused on a goal that one hardly sees anything else. In fact, focus and determination are the necessary elements needed to achieve any kind of result, and they are the mainstays of success.

When you were a child, did you ever use a magnifying glass to focus the sun's rays and burn up a blade of grass? We can liken our own directed focus to the same powerful effect the magnifying glass has on a ray of sunshine. So why do we need flexibility? When we are *too* focused, we become rigid and unyielding and unable to ride life's irritable, bumpy roads. Can we *be* both focused and flexible at the same time? Not only can we, but we *must* be. We must find a balancing point between having enough focus to accomplish our goals without giving up, and enough flexibility to ride out the obstacles, taking in stride the disappointments we encounter along the way. Just as our bodies need to be stretched to remain pliable and to reduce injuries, so do our minds and our hearts.

Confidence and humility – The second oxymoron of life is that of finding balance between confidence and humility. Being confident and successful means we need to love ourselves unconditionally. We must recognize that each of us is good and that we have unique talents and traits. People who are able to love themselves fully are able to love others. Their confidence extends beyond their own lives into the lives of everyone else they touch.

There is nothing wrong with loving oneself. There is nothing braggadocio or big-headed about it, although many of us were taught to believe so by our parents and grandparents. Keep in mind, though, that loving oneself does not mean eliminating the need to continue to improve. People who truly love themselves are free to move forward, to identify their unique talents, and to achieve great success with their own individuality.

At the same time we are loving ourselves unconditionally, we must also be humble. We must recognize that a greater order exists, and while we do control a good part of our own destiny, we do not have complete power over everything in our lives. This is a lesson taught by those who formed Alcoholics Anonymous. According to this highly successful group and program, when there is a problem, we must recognize that we may be powerless over it and that healing and success come only when we allow acceptance of this larger order.

Although they may appear contradictory, having both confident humility and humble confidence is important to our success. A person with healthy self-esteem can be humble, and a truly humble person can be confident in his or her own specialness.

Recently Steven Spielberg, commenting on his feeling of success after the movie *Schindler's List,* said, "I don't have to prove anything to anyone anymore. I don't have to prove anything to myself. I just have to keep myself interested."

Honesty and hope – It takes a great deal of courage to be brutally honest about life and about ourselves. It takes courage and chutzpah to face the world for what it is, accepting both the positives and the negatives. On the other hand, it is equally important to remain hopeful.

*"Hope is the pillar that holds up the world.
Hope is the dream of the waking man."*
— PLINY THE ELDER

So how is it possible to find the necessary balance between honesty and hope? There are many examples of this from the field of medicine. I particularly enjoy the writings of Norman Cousins. In his book, *Head First,* he quotes an anecdote regarding hope submitted by William Bucholz, M.D.:

> As I was eating breakfast one morning, I overheard two oncologists discussing the papers they were to present that day at the national meeting of the American Society of Clinical Oncology. One was complaining bitterly. "You know, Bob, I just don't understand it. We use the same drugs, the same dosage, the same schedule, and the same entry criteria. Yet, I got a 22% response rate and you got a 74%. That's unheard of for metastatic lung cancer. How do you do it?" The other doctor replied, "We're both using etoposide, platinol, oncovin, and hydroxyurea. You call yours EPOH. But I tell my patients I'm giving them HOPE. Sure, I tell them this is experimental and we go over the long list of side effects together. But I emphasize that we have a chance. As dismal as the statistics are for non-small cell, there are always a few percent who do really well."

Medical research is replete with examples of hopeful people who have better recovery rates than those who are more pessimistic. It takes great chutzpah to retain hope when things seem at their worst, but this is precisely the most important time to do so. Keep in mind that being hopeful does not mean we should be dishonest with, nor fool ourselves about, what

87

may be going on in our lives. What it does mean is that we *choose* optimism over pessimism. Chutzy people are optimists, which is why they are successful. As the automobile manufacturer Henry Ford once said, "Whether you think you can or you think you can't, you are right. If you choose to look at the world as hopeless, then you are right. If, however, you choose to look at the world full of hope, wonder and optimism, then you are also correct. It is your choice."

Patience and persistence – How is it possible to be both patient and persistent? Doesn't patience mean waiting things out? And doesn't persistence, conversely, mean not waiting but continuing on, step by step, no matter what? The secret to maintaining the balance between these contradictory terms is to continue to work toward a goal, staying focused on the outcome, while at the same time allowing that all things happen in good time. Being patient takes a great deal of strength, whether you are eagerly pursuing your own success or waiting for the success of others.

With whom do we need to be patient? We need to be patient with our coworkers, our bosses, our family members, our friends, our lovers and, indeed, ourselves. Some people bloom later than others and mature according to their own timetable. We learn this from watching our children grow and develop. Even those in the same family develop at different rates, and boys can certainly develop differently from girls. I had to learn this in a painful way myself.

As a child, I had always been very eager to read. I remember being four years old and trying to read everything I could. I'd spend most mornings more interested in reading the cereal box than in eating the cereal. Reading was something that came easily and naturally to me, and I expected the same from others around me. So I was thrown quite a curve when my one and only son seemed unable to read. It appeared he had a *reading problem,* his grade school teachers continuously reminded me. John's low grades were a result of his *reading problem.* John had trouble with his homework because of his *reading problem.* John appeared less-than-intelligent because of his *reading problem.* I was helping him every night with his homework, and I was becoming less and less patient with his inability to read at the level I thought he should. Finally, after the fifth grade, I took him to a professional reading evaluator at the local university. I am thankful every day for the advice I was given.

After a two-hour test, the evaluator dismissed John from the room and called me in to speak with her. She refused to call him a child with a *reading problem.* She said there was nothing wrong with him; that developmentally he was just about six months behind the rest of the children his age, and that he would probably catch up by the seventh grade. She said his only problem was that I, his mother, had been referring to it as a *reading problem.*

I was ashamed to discover that I was potentially sabotaging my own child's success because of my lack of patience with his development. So he wasn't like me. Did he need to be? An amazing thing happened as a result of all this. I stopped using the term *reading problem* and delightedly told John that he was just fine and that he would catch up in no time. He went to summer school that year with his head held higher than I had seen in a long while. By the time he reached the eighth grade, he did catch up. He is not yet reading Tolstoy (but then, neither am I), but he calls himself a great reader. I learned a valuable lesson from this whole experience; that patience is more than a great virtue. It is a necessity for success.

But patience does not mean sitting back while watching and waiting for things to happen. Nor is it synonymous with procrastination and putting things off because they are unpleasant. It *does* mean being proactive. No matter what your goal, you still have to keep plugging away while realizing that it takes time and patience to achieve those successes. Persistence is the flip side of patience, and it is the number one trait shared by successful people.

Someone who knew all about the important relationship of patience and persistence was baseball legend Babe Ruth. Most of us are not aware that Babe Ruth retains the strike-out record. What we remember is the number of home runs he hit. Babe Ruth knew that when he picked up the bat and faced the pitcher, he would most likely strike out. But even armed with this statistical certainty, he persisted. Today he is known for his home runs, not his strikeouts.

Perhaps you do not believe the old saying that good things come to those who wait. You may instead prefer the quote of Thomas Edison who said, "Everything comes to him who *hustles* while he waits." Whatever your beliefs, know that persistence and patience make things happen.

Finding Balance Between the Oxymorons of Life

IF OXYMORONS ARE an ever-present symbol of our lives, how do we find the balance between such contradictory notions? Isn't it true that through pain, we appreciate pleasure, through fear that we appreciate security, and through loss that we appreciate what and who we have? In searching for this balance, we can learn some lessons from the martial arts.

The purpose of the early training steps in kenpo karate, a form of martial arts, is to show the student that when he has his balance, his opponent cannot be balanced. Students are told that this theory extends into all aspects of their lives.

"When you practice your techniques, think about

how you are gaining your balance and what is happening to your opponent. This will give you some insight on how some people seem to never be bothered by what others do.

If you have balance in your job, you know what you are expected to do and manage to meet the deadline. In your home life you have obligations and as long as you meet them, you have balance and your home is your sanctuary. The next time you feel like things are out of control, look at yourself, gain your balance, and your obstacle will not have control.

This principle of maintaining balance is the same as the Alcoholics Anonymous credo of changing the things that you can and accepting the things that you can't. While this may be a difficult way to look at life, it is the best way to gain your balance and control your own destiny. The most important lesson is that you must wait for an action before you can react with any degree of accuracy. In our lives we all anticipate the actions of others and many times we lose our balance with this anticipation, because others do not act on our anticipation, they act on their own. If you remain ready to react without anticipation, you will find that you will not be caught off balance. This way of living will increase your enjoyment of things around you."

(*Kenpo Karate Newsletter,* January, 1994)

The Alcoholics Anonymous creed referred to earlier states: "Grant me the serenity to accept the things I cannot change, the courage to change the things I can, and the wisdom to know the difference." Our lives are in balance when we know that difference. Of course, some of you may prefer the modified version, "Grant me the serenity to accept the things I cannot change, the courage to change the things I can, and the wisdom to hide the bodies of those people I had to kill because they pissed me off." And remember, humor is an important way to keep balance.

To keep our balance, we must constantly evaluate the things we believe to be the most important. To have more balance in our lives, we must do the following:

- Know who we are
- Love who we are
- Be focused and flexible
- Have confidence and humility
- Remain honest and hopeful
- Be persistent and patient
- Live our lives fully with all things in moderation

Balance and Rhythm in the Most Unlikely Places

MY UNCLE GUS was one of the most balanced people I have ever known, but you might not know that by looking at him, for Uncle Gus had a limp. He sustained an unrepaired war injury during World War II which affected his hip. The older he got, the shorter the affected leg became, and his limp became more and more pronounced. It would appear that he was a rather unbalanced man if you saw him walking down the street, and you would think I was an unbalanced child if you saw me following this wonderful man I loved, imitating his limp as accurately as I could. But I was not the only one to love Gus; everyone who knew him did. He was a loving and generous man who touched the lives of many.

When Uncle Gus died recently at the young age of 82, I, like all of his friends and family, felt saddened and out-of-balance. For you see, Uncle Gus was everybody's uncle. He was always there to offer a big smile, a kind word, and a nonjudgmental loan.

At the simple gravesite service, the young rabbi offered some thoughts which helped restore the sense of balance in our hearts. "When a person dies, God asks him three questions about his life. If he can answer 'yes' to all three of them, then he has lived a good life – a balanced life – and it is okay for him to go."

The first question is, "Did he procreate for this earth?" By this, God does not necessarily mean having children. This was a good thing, for Uncle Gus never had any children of his own. He didn't need to. All who came in contact with Uncle Gus felt wrapped in his love, the way a child would feel enveloped by the arms of a loving parent. Uncle Gus loved all of his family unconditionally, never thought a bad thought about anyone, and nurtured us constantly.

According to the rabbi, the next question God asks is, "Was he honest in his business dealings?" As you will note, Jews are very practical, even in their final thoughts. Uncle Gus was, indeed, honest in his business dealings. During the Depression, he helped in my grandfather's store to distribute bread to poor people who had no means. Uncle Gus always gave more than he expected to get, and he was considered honest by everyone.

The third question God asks is, "Did he enjoy all that the world and this life had to offer?" And boy, did he! Uncle Gus loved his food, his friends, his simple life, his trips to the mall, his visits from the family. And he especially enjoyed his "four fingers" (a way to measure good whiskey).

These questions show the importance of balance. Working hard, creating for the earth, being honest in all dealings, and enjoying all that this life has to offer is the ultimate in balance. Uncle Gus was certainly a symbol of this balance, for he lived a good, if shortened, life.

The Talmud says: "In the world to come, each of us will be asked to account for all the good things God put on earth which we failed to enjoy." There is so much for us to enjoy. Success comes from finding balance among all these things. Success is finding balance in an unbalanced world, like finding beauty and rhythm in the limp of your favorite uncle.

9

Trait #6:

Give and Give Back

*"Some think they have made a success of life,
when all they've made is a lot of money."*

When John Fitzgerald Kennedy challenged us to, "Ask not what your country can do for you, ask what you can do for your country," he was describing the psychology of giving, that idea of giving to others while expecting nothing in return. The benefit of giving, also found in the Bible as "breads cast upon the waters," is supported by recent research showing the healthful results of giving.

In a study of volunteers, it was found that people who give have something wonderful in their blood. They found increased levels of endorphins – nature's pain killer. These are the same endorphins and exhilirating feelings you get from runner's high. Isn't that amazing? Some of us who don't run can get that feeling just by giving and giving back. I call it "nature's natural margarita."

To be successful you must give and give before you get and get. There are many times when it feels like you are giving all the giving and not getting the getting. But that isn't true at all. When you are giving, you feel good. In order to have more chutzpah, you have to give without expectation of getting. However, you will always *get* a whole lot more than you *give.*

Eugene Lange

THE STORY OF EUGENE LANGE clearly illustrates the benefits of giving and giving back. Eugene was a poor man from East Harlem who had gone to college to pursue a degree in social work. Instead, he found he had a knack for making money. So, this once-poor man became a rich industrialist. One day many years later, he was preparing to give a graduation speech to a group of poor, inner-city sixth-graders. Sitting there with his speech in his hand, he was about to tell them about the value of hard work and how they, too, could achieve the "American Dream." But something came over him. In a moment of pure chutzpah, he stood up to the podium, took out his speech, and ripped it to shreds. Then he looked out on those little faces, those young, promising, yet doubtful faces, and said: "Here's what I'm going to do. I'm going to put money into an account for each of you, and when you finish high school, I will pay for you to go to college." When I asked Mr. Lange how he felt about making that promise that day, he said to me, "It only hurt for a minute. And then it felt really good!"

Eugene Lange then founded the "I Have A Dream Foundation" and has financed the education of many children from the inner city since that day. He changed their lives and also changed his own. He has amazingly increased the rate of inner city children graduating from high school and earning higher degrees. And boy, does he feel good.

There are many ways to give, whether with money or without. Eugene Lange gave in both ways. He knew these children needed his attention in addition to his money, so he put together classes to help them improve their SAT and other precollege entrance scores. He also took a personal interest in them. He invited them to his downtown office to meet him, and he – this very busy industrialist – would talk to them personally and tell them how much he believed in them, showing interest in their lives. That's something we all can do without spending a dime. We can give of ourselves. We can be mentors.

To have more chutzpah, sometimes we need to *find* a mentor. And at other times we need to *be* a mentor. We reach our next level by helping others reach their next level. We are successful when they succeed. One person who taught us about mentoring was Bill Wilson, the founder of Alcoholics Anonymous. Bill W. found that the best way to heal himself and succeed was to help other people heal and succeed. The AA premise is founded on, among other things, being available to help others. Because when we help, we heal.

The notion of giving without getting is universal in scope. The Russians say, "If every person will give one thread, the poor man will soon have a coat." And the Chinese say, "A little bit of the fragrance rests on the hand of he who gives the roses." We get a lot more chutzpah when we give, give, give than when we look to get, get, get.

Ondra

BUT WHAT CAN YOU GIVE if you are black and poor? That is how Ondra was born in 1958 and how he lived most of his youth in depressed East St. Louis. As a child, he saw a great deal of crime and violence in a community that had been abandoned by businesses, and in which many people were without work, finances, and food. There were open displays of gunfire, and many children in his grammar school died at an early age.

For Ondra, it was all about survival. He remembers eating beans every day – and in every different way – fried beans, mashed beans, baked beans, pinto beans. But he was tough and became a "hard-core kid." Hunger will do that to a young man. He was so hungry that he prayed for food, and one day he actually dove for a candy bar he saw in a garbage can. Many days he could only take half a sandwich to school. His family was so poor that he could not afford tennis shoes and, therefore, could not take gym class. What a shame for a young, beautiful, athletic black boy in the mid-1960's to be unable to participate in sports.

Then a school busing program started relocating many of the black students to a white school. Most of the children adapted quickly, but Ondra would not. He was tough and defiant and was sent every day to the principal for all sorts of infractions. But the principal liked Ondra and soon they were buddies. Ondra even told him how to detect the difference between cigarette and marijuana smoke in the bathrooms. The principal put Ondra into a different class where the teacher, Mr. Marsh, took a special interest in him.

Mr. Marsh took Ondra to his own home, fed him, and even bought him tennis shoes. Mr. Marsh believed in him and helped turn the young man around. When Ondra graduated from high school, it was with great pride. No one in his family had accomplished that feat before. It was an even bigger celebration because Ondra had earned a scholarship to a private college, a scholarship for both academic and athletic achievement. You see, those tennis shoes that Mr. Marsh bought helped Ondra jump high and run fast.

But college wasn't easy for Ondra, as he lacked knowledge in many of the basic core subjects. He had to attend summer school every year in order to complete college in the required four years. But complete it he did, with a degree in education and with plans to be a schoolteacher.

Shortly after graduation, Ondra moved with his fiancee to Reno, Nevada, but there were no teaching positions open. The police department, however, was hiring and it paid much better. The $18,000 starting salary sounded like a windfall to Ondra. So, with no prior experience or interest in police work, he enrolled in the academy and became one of the first black officers in the Reno police department.

Today, Deputy Chief Ondra Berry is a special police liaison to the at-risk youth in the community, working with youth and gangs. He talks to them in their schools and in their neighborhoods, and is a role model of success for all deprived children and children of color.

Deputy Chief Berry attributes most of his success to the positive influences of his teacher, Mr. Marsh, and to his grandmother, who made him go to church. Ondra has developed a very deep spiritual nature and a real respect for that which is bigger than himself. Through his work at the church, he has learned the importance of giving.

"God tests me a lot," he says. "I have been put in many situations which are challenging, demanding, and sometimes frightening." He was frightened of public speaking until his grandmother forced him to give speeches in church. Now he relishes the opportunity to give presentations and to work with youth one-on-one and in groups. He believes in the power of the positive role model. He knows how mentors can turn one's life around and he intends to repay the debt by being a mentor himself.

God may test Ondra Berry a lot, but he seems to be passing those tests with flying colors.

By the way, Ondra no longer eats beans.

The Gift

THERE ARE MANY WAYS to give, and it sometimes becomes blurred as to who is the giver and who is the givee.

It was the last day before Christmas vacation and my son John's seventh grade class was planning an outing. They needed parents to chaperone. Because I'm *self*-employed, my son figures I am *un*employed, with a schedule flexible enough to allow me to attend many of his activities. I reluctantly agreed but was not excited about where the class was going. They were off for a Christmas visit to the Long-Care Hospital, also known as the old folks' home.

That December morning was cold and gray; so was the hospital. When our group arrived, we were greeted by only a couple of staff members. The holiday decorations displayed around the facility were meager, and their attempt to liven up the surroundings only made the dreariness more pronounced.

The children were to visit the patients with certain welcoming signs on their nightstands. Each student had made a craft gift and a card to give to an elderly patient. Now, I don't like these places. Ever since I was a child and had to visit my mother's Aunt Goldie in a home in California, I had hoped I would never have to return to one. There is a certain feel and smell about such places that is very upsetting to me. But I tried to be a good sport and a good role model for the children. I helped them find their appointed gift recipient, but I avoided making any direct contact with the patients myself.

After about 20 minutes, when all of the children had found their designated people and had passed out the holiday goodies, I found myself wandering the hall alone. I really wanted to escape, but I knew we had another hour-and-a-half there, so I decided to make the best of it. About that time, I passed a patient's doorway and looked in. The old woman lying in the bed had no placard indicating she was up for visitors, but she seemed lively and alert and eager for a visit. I walked in slowly. "Hi, I'm Idora. Merry Christmas, and how are you doing?"

The old woman turned her head and looked at me slowly. She had long grayish-white hair and steely gray-blue eyes. At first, she looked to me like a witch, and she had that smell. I felt like Gretl in *Hansel and Gretl* and wanted to bolt. But then the woman smiled and took my hand in hers. I was amazed at how soft hers was. "My name is Evelyn," she said. "I'm 92 years old and I'm waiting for Sweet Jesus to take me so I can join my husband in heaven. Do you have a husband?" She patted the bedside next to her for me to sit.

"I had a husband once," I told her, "but it didn't work out. My beautiful son brought me here today with his school. He is the light of my life." For some strange reason, I started to tell Evelyn the story of my life. She asked when my birthday was, and when I told her the date, she said it was the same as her brother's. She said I was a good woman and deserving of a good man. I asked her how she knew all this and she responded that although she couldn't hear well and her vision was failing, she could tell a great deal about a person from holding her hand.

We held hands and talked for a long time, exchanging stories about our lives. She told me she had been in this hospital much too long and couldn't wait to leave. She wondered if, in fact, I would be willing to put her in my car and take her downtown. She really missed the lights of the casinos, and said she would love to go gambling.

I didn't know how much of Evelyn's story to believe. A lot of what she said made sense, but at other times she seemed to be living in another world. Nevertheless, she and I made a very deep connection that day, and it was with surprising sadness when it came time for me to leave. I was pleased to have given an old woman some diversion from the dull existence of her final days, but she gave me something also.

On Christmas Eve, my son always goes to the home of his father and stepmother to celebrate the holiday. But on the 23rd, he stays with me. "What shall we do tonight, John?" I asked him after dinner.

"Mommy, why don't we go back to the old people's home and bring them some more gifts. It's getting close to Christmas and I think they are lonely," he replied. If I had ever wondered about the kind of child I was rearing, I no longer had to worry. Any child with that big a heart and gracious a spirit...

When we arrived at the hospital toting gifts and cookies, the scene was quite different from that of the other morning. Instead of the patients being clean, medicated, and tucked into their beds, they were in their wheelchairs pouring slowly to and from the cafeteria for dinner. The smell was still there, only worse this time.

We finally found Evelyn, stuck alone in the corner of the cafeteria. She remembered me and asked me to wheel her back to her room. John, in the meantime, was playing Santa Claus, passing out the trinkets and cookies to everyone he could find. Evelyn was glad we had returned, although somewhat surprised. After getting her back into bed, we held hands and talked for a long time. She told me not to worry about life because I would have a good one. She advised me never to hook up with a man again unless he was as good as her dearly beloved husband. She asked me again to put her in my car and take her downtown. I told her maybe next time.

That night was the last time I saw Evelyn. The hospital was sold very soon thereafter, and all the patients were transferred to other locations. I don't know what happened to her. All the staff left and I could find no record. I'm not even sure she gave me her correct name.

Christmas held a special meaning for me that year. I learned another aspect of giving beyond what I had already known. I have always considered myself to have a great deal of Christmas spirit, which is especially exciting since I am Jewish! Evelyn gave me a deep appreciation of the elderly. She helped eradicate the fears I had of attending to old, dying people, and I will always thank her for that. I don't know where she is now, but I hope that she is safely in the arms of her beloved husband.

It takes great chutzpah to find creative ways to give. To be successful, we must give and give back in order to pass along our gifts and talents to others. Eugene Lange gives money and time to underprivileged children. Ondra Berry gives them hope and inspiration.

Keep your eyes and hearts open for opportunities to give. Give to people you have nothing in common with and see how you feel. Giving and getting are so intricately entwined that it is usually hard to tell the difference. No matter what your religion or beliefs, the Christmas spirit lives in all of us. Why wait for December 25th?

10

Trait #7:

Grow
New Eyes

*"The only difference between stumbling blocks
and stepping stones is the way you use them."*

Part of the process of success requires growing new eyes, or in other words, getting a new outlook on life.
It means taking a look at the past, letting go, and forgiving the
hurts or injustices that serve no purpose other than to get in
the way of your current quest for success. Growing new eyes
means discovering what is really important in life. It means
reframing your goals and seeing them in a different light. In
some cases, it may be one particular event in our lives that
helps us to see the world differently, which is exactly what happened to me in the late fall of 1990.

I was outside a hotel in Las Vegas, with three heavy bags full
of seminar materials. There were no attendants or bellmen
available to help me move them, so, in my impatience, I bent
over and picked up all three bags at once. Suddenly, I felt an
unfamiliar twinge in my lower back and knew I was in trouble.
Within a couple of days, the pain had become unbearable.
Then my right leg curled up and went numb. I had blown a
disk in my lower back. When the neurosurgeon told me I

would need back surgery, I was terrified. Because of my background in medical malpractice, I feared major surgery. I had seen many cases of death and disability result from serious surgeries, and I was afraid the same thing could happen to me.

Here I was, a single mother, loving and supporting a young son. I was in business for myself. There was my beautiful office downtown with lucrative contracts, a full staff, and lots of promise. I feared not surviving this surgery, but I also feared the more real possibility of disability.

On the morning of the surgery, as I was being wheeled away in preparation for the operation, I said good-bye to my friends and family with more fear than I had ever known; the fear that I might never see them again. I was the only patient awaiting surgery in that hospital basement, and I was lonely as I lay there waiting for the anesthesiologist. When he finally arrived and met me for the first time, he danced around my bed but never made eye contact with me. Finally, I looked at him and whispered, "You know, I am very scared." I guess he didn't want to deal with a scared human being, so he flicked a switch and I was out cold.

The next thing I remember, I was waking up and looking at the clock on the wall. It was 11:10 a.m. I knew the surgery must be over because I had gone in before 9:00 a.m. By all appearances, I had made it through. I looked down at my right leg and wiggled my foot. It worked! As a wave of joy poured over me, I felt very thankful to be alive and to have a healthy leg and foot. I said to myself, "Idora, you are alive, and everything seems to be working. Anything that happens to you now will just be *inconvenience.*" And there have been plenty of inconveniences.

Back Surgery Improved My Vision

IT TOOK ME ABOUT SIX MONTHS to recover from surgery. I closed the office, moved it to my home, and gave up all my contracts. And I had absolutely nothing. On the one hand, I was terrified. I wondered what I was going to do, where my next dollar was going to come from, and how I was going to support myself and my son. On the other hand, I felt this great *freedom.* For the first time in my life, I felt free to go in whatever direction happened along, to pursue whatever opportunities or interests came my way. I asked myself, "What am I feeling so free about?" An amazing thing had happened. Back surgery cleared up my *eyesight!* It helped me to see what was really important in my life. And I discovered that it wasn't the big office downtown, the lucrative contracts or the fancy business suits. What was important was living day-to-day, loving the people around me, appreciating family and friends and knowing that when we are really in touch with ourselves and our talents, everything will be okay. While I knew I had a long recuperation ahead of me, I now saw the world as full of *possibilities* instead of full of *problems.*

It was good that my vision had improved and that I had grown my new eyes, for the world, indeed, started to look different. I could have lamented the fact that I had to close my office and give up the contracts for which I had worked so hard. I could have been sad and depressed. In fact, I *should* have been sad and depressed. Instead, I felt truly blessed to be able to see the world in a different light, and this new perception has helped me to reach another level in my development. My new eyes helped me to redefine success. It no longer was the trappings of the downtown office; it was the ability to walk on my own two feet, to finally drive my own car, to look into the eyes of my child, and to look forward to starting life all over.

When the first round of physical therapy was complete, I began thinking about work again. Starting over would be quite a challenge, but not nearly as tough as the one I had just survived. With my old outlook, I might have considered myself a failure, somebody who took a chance with her health and almost completely screwed up her life. But with my new eyesight, I did not see the world that way at all. Instead, I adopted a line from a Janis Joplin song as my new motto: "Freedom's just another word for nothing left to lose..." I felt that I had nothing left to lose because I was alive and I had my health, my friends, and my family. So onward I marched, limping a little at first, but climbing toward a new rung on my ladder of success.

Jimmy

Many successful people grow new eyes at some time in their lives. Indeed, in the blink of an eye, our view can change and can substantially alter or reinforce our values. And sometimes it becomes necessary to grow new eyes when a situation is so painful that emotional survival is in question. Let me tell you the story of Jimmy/Jay.

Jimmy was born November 17, 1944. He had been adopted by a single woman during his first year of life, a fact which was always made very clear to him. He lived with his mother and grandmother in a beautiful, spacious home in rural New Jersey. He was reared in the fine eastern tradition of wealth and sophistication. The family traveled abroad and entertained extensively. His mother loved him, yet she was stern and distant. His nanny, Loleta, was Jimmy's main source of comfort and attention throughout his childhood years. He had no doubt that his family and Loleta all loved him, but for some reason he always felt different.

Jimmy was an intelligent, curious child who had many questions about his heritage. He asked his mother about his birth parents, but she merely told him that his father had been killed during World War II and his mother died shortly after his birth. The only other information she offered Jimmy was the fact that she had left her own parents' home several months before his birth and returned home to New Jersey with him when he was almost one year old. Jimmy wanted to know more, but his mother considered the subject closed and would say nothing more about it. Jimmy, however, would always continue to wonder. When he was five years old, Jimmy's name was changed to Jay in memory of his adoptive mother's father.

As Jay grew older and started to rebel a bit, his mother found it increasingly difficult to handle him. Her main tactic of discipline was to feign a heart attack by leaning against the wall and fanning herself with her hand. At first, this ruse would frighten Jay, but over time it began to anger him.

At the age of 13, Jay was sent to a private boarding school, where his rebellion grew. He lost interest in his studies and started to get into trouble. Consequently, his mother moved him to a special boarding school for children with emotional problems. In his senior year, just as Jay was becoming more comfortable with himself and was turning himself around, his mother moved him out of this boarding school and into yet another one. Her reason for doing so was that she feared he would play football, a game and an image she could not tolerate. In addition to that, she didn't want Jay to graduate from a "special school."

Jay Sees the Truth

BY NOW JAY WAS FURIOUS. His life continued to be filled with more secrets and confusion. Then one day Jay was studying the picture of his mother's father, after whom he had been renamed. He looked at the man's face in the painting which was prominently displayed over the mantle in the living room. He then looked in the mirror at his own. The resemblance was unmistakable. A startling realization slowly came over him. He was *indeed* part of this family. The terrible secret that had hovered over him all his life had to be that he was *not* adopted, but was, in fact, his mother's natural child.

So who was his father, and how did all this happen? And why wouldn't his mother share the truth with him? Jay's young but active mind clicked sequences together, and he formed his own theory of what might have happened. His mother must have gotten pregnant out of wedlock. During World War II, this was still a terrible transgression and a difficult thing for a family of breeding to accept and announce. She must have fallen in love with somebody when she worked in New York. A soldier, maybe? Perhaps the pregnancy was an accident, and she then devised this elaborate scheme to make it appear as though she had adopted the child instead of giving birth to him. And how many people knew of this? Did his grandparents know? Did his nanny know? Maybe it hadn't been an accident at all. Maybe his mother knew she would never marry, but got herself pregnant on purpose so she could rear a child of her own. No man had ever presented himself to the family to claim paternity. So why all the secrets? Why couldn't his mother trust him enough to tell him the truth? Why did he have to grow up thinking that he was an outsider?

Jay's anger boiled into fury. At first, he considered confronting his mother. He wanted to yell at her and accuse her of sin and adultery and mistreatment. But then something came over him. In that moment, he grew new eyes. He decided that her secret would remain her secret. He would allow her to continue her life as it was because it obviously was important to her. And in that moment when Jay grew new eyes, he also grew from a child to a man. He chose to keep this secret within himself so as not to destroy his mother's illusion of the happy family. A chutzy deed, indeed. The new eyesight Jay gained when he saw his own face reflected in the portrait of his mother's father would never allow him to see the world the same again.

After his discovery, life for Jay was not easy. He didn't know what to believe about his mother or his family. He was disturbed, uncertain and insecure. He barely made it through high school and then went out into the work world. He married young and fathered a child by the age of 20. The young boy was beautiful and affectionate, but the marriage was not destined to last. Jay made the decision to leave everything behind him, and moved west to Reno, Nevada.

Moving out from under his mother's wing was good for Jay. Slowly and painfully, he began to mature and to become more comfortable with himself. He enjoyed a myriad of different jobs. He even drove a cab, taking customers to the local house of prostitution. For Jay, it was a fun life, but not very meaningful. So he enrolled in the university, worked his way through college, and remarried. Graduating from college was a monumental point of success for Jay. He had never quite achieved anything before, and the feeling of accomplishment brought on by his own perseverance felt wonderful. Several years later, Jay took the next step and enrolled in law school, and three years after that, went to work for the district attorney's office.

He struggled to make ends meet and was very discouraged when he did not pass the bar examination the first time. But he had learned the lesson of perseverance. He took the test again and passed.

But problems continued to plague Jay. Certain feelings of anger and resentment toward his mother lingered, and they were taking their toll on him and his relationships with other people. Jay felt the time had come to visit his mother, and so he returned to New Jersey in 1984. On the last day of his week-long visit, his mother decided to reveal the truth. Sitting under the picture of Jay's grandfather, his mother told Jay that the man in the portrait was his natural grandfather, and that she was his birth mother. Before Jay could recover from the shock of his mother's admission and ask all the questions he had held inside himself his entire life, the driver arrived to take Jay to the airport. She would say no more on the topic.

The next time Jay saw his mother was on Christmas Eve of 1985. She was very ill and in the hospital. They talked of love. Jay's mother had grown very proud of him, although she wasn't sure how she had earned the love of this very courageous young man. Tears flowed silently down her cheeks. She held his hand, closed her eyes and nodded in understanding. Jay's mother then suffered a massive heart attack. She was momentarily revived, but slipped into a coma. Jay left the hospital room and returned to his hotel. By the time he got there, his mother was dead.

Part of the truth about his heritage had been revealed, but Jay would never learn the rest, for his mother had been the last remaining person in the family who knew all the facts. He had harbored his mother's deep, dark secret for many years, probably to his own detriment. But now with his new eyes, Jay saw his mother for the human being she was – an imperfect one, with many secrets and fears – and he realized he no longer had to walk in her shadow. He was his own man and would make of his life what he could. And that he has.

Jay went to work as an attorney, taking many chutzy steps to move his career along. At some point, he decided to become a judge. He ran for office, and he and his wife stumped the neighborhoods campaigning. He spent a great deal of his own money, as well as the small inheritance he had received from his mother, in his bid for election; and he made it. Little Jimmy/Jay became a judge and continues on in that position to this date.

Through the Eyes of Others

THERE ARE MANY TIMES when we feel powerless to take control of the important aspects in our lives. These are the times when we must use chutzpah to force the growth of new eyes. It takes chutzpah to purposely turn a negative situation into a positive one, and to take control once again. It takes chutzpah to learn from a failure. In a previous chapter, I discussed the notion that nothing is a failure if we ask the following: What were the lessons learned and the gifts received? When we have the chutzpah to turn a failure into a learning and giving experience, we are forcing the growth of new eyes. We are choosing to see the world differently and to reassert our control.

Sometimes it takes the outlook of someone else to help us to see more clearly.

Kathy

SOME YEARS AGO, when I was just out of college and in my early 20's, I worked with a young girl at an insurance company in Sacramento, California. Her name was Kathy and she was 19 years old. She had a three-year-old son, an infirm alcoholic mother, and a ne'er-do-well, unsupporting husband. I was a somewhat cynical and critical college graduate. Kathy, on the other hand, was a very positive young woman. One day, I asked her, "How do you do all this? How do you raise your little boy, take care of your mother after work, and still arrive here every day with a smile on your face? And why do you let that husband come in and out of your life at his pleasure?"

What Kathy said to me made me ashamed of myself. "You know, life isn't so bad. In fact, it's good. My little apartment will be just fine for awhile and it will look much better when I get finished painting it. I love spending time with my mother even though she is cranky and ill-tempered. She is my mother and I want to be with her during her difficult time. My husband is a young man, and I'm sure he will find his way back to us sometime."

Kathy was a beautiful young woman with an even more beautiful spirit and approach. I decided that I wanted to adopt her attitude toward life. I thought that if Kathy could face her challenges with poise, dignity and chutzpah, then I was in no position to be so negative about mine. When I became determined to look at the world the way Kathy did, I grew new eyes for myself, and I have been ever pleased with that decision. I purposely have positive friends and try to look at the world in terms of what is right instead of what is wrong. It is not always easy.

Recently, I had a dramatic downturn in my business. After four years of rebuilding my client base after my surgery, day-by-day, project-by-project, speech-by-speech, there came a time when, all at once, nearly all my clients either went out of business, moved, went in a different direction, or had management upheavals. At first I was discouraged, depressed, and felt a little sorry for myself. Again, I was worried. How would I support my son and my business? How could all this happen at one time? What had I done? How long would it take to again rebuild my business?

I moped around, muttering to myself. Then finally one day I had the *"ah ha!"* feeling of realization that comes with growing new eyes. There was nothing wrong with my business, I had just gone on a *sabbatical.* A sabbatical is something I had always wanted to take but had never had time for. Usually people plan and prepare for their sabbatical, but mine just happened, and it occurred to me that it had just happened for a good reason. It was time for me to write this book. I had been planning, preparing, and talking about it for two years, but would probably never have started unless I had a big gaping hole in my work schedule. So with a hearty laugh, a new pep in my step and a fresh outlook, I redefined my business downturn as my book-writing sabbatical!

Reframing Turns Negatives into Positives

WHAT I DID IN THIS INSTANCE was to grow new eyes by using a strategy called *reframing.* Reframing is the conscious decision to redefine incidents or situations to make them more positive. Think of the purpose that a frame serves around a picture. The size, position and shape of the frame helps direct our eye to things in the picture. By changing the size, angle, color or shape of the frame, we can redirect our attention to different aspects of what is inside the frame. So it is with our view of the world. By changing the frame – or the way we view events, people, and situations – we can change our perspective. Reframing is a very powerful technique we can use to grow new eyes in order to change our perceptions of our past, our present and, indeed, our future.

When my sister and I get together and inevitably discuss

events in our past, we are shocked, amused, and sometimes dismayed at the different ways in which we remember the same story or incident. Sometimes our variation in memories is laughable; other times it is frightening. When we add the recollection of our brother to the mix, the truth of the past becomes even more clouded.

The current trend in facing one's past and using support groups to gain new perspective is laudable. Many people have distressing pasts. Many have been abused by family members, brought up with neglect, fear, and poverty. Many of these same individuals are having trouble in their current lives because of the problems in their past. If there are things in your past which are throwing up roadblocks to your success, then you may need to reframe them. Some children of abusive or neglectful parents become despondent, unproductive adults who continue a cycle of neglect or abuse, while others go on to overcome these deficiencies and become healthy, happy, successful individuals. In some cases, differences in personal temperament help people accept challenges and move on. Others are unable to do that. But another reason for the difference in outcomes is the way people choose to look at their pasts. You can choose to blame your past for your current difficulties, or you can choose to move on.

In his book, *You'll See It When You Believe It*, author Wayne Dyer recounts the story of how his own past affected him. Wayne's father had abandoned his young family, and Wayne never saw him again. He grew up to have trouble in relationships, was unable to hold a job, and had a myriad of other behavioral problems. He blamed all of this on his father. Because he didn't have a good father figure influence in his life, he felt he was just marking time and would never be successful.

Dyer tells the very touching story of how he happened upon the grave of his father long after his death and how he stood there yelling and screaming about the problems he had caused Wayne in his life. Suddenly, he says, after about an hour of this tirade, Wayne grew new eyes (my words, not his). He suddenly realized that his father was just a human being like everyone else, that he had problems of his own, and that he needed to be forgiven. So Wayne forgave him. That moment of revelation changed Wayne for the good.

After that incident, he finally took hold of his own life, stopped blaming his father, and went on to amazing accomplishments in the field of psychology and psychotherapy. He authored a number of best-selling motivational books and is an inspiration to successful people throughout the world. This came from an *"ah ha"* moment which changed him forever. In viewing his father as a fallible human being, Wayne was able to reframe the events of his past and thereby reframe his own future.

Kathleen's New Eye(s)

MY FRIEND KATHLEEN from Chapter 1, who screamed at the nurses to get the pain medication for her eye, eventually lost that eye in service to our government. It was a frightening and painful experience for her to learn that, at the age of 25, her right eye would be practically useless and that her left eye would have to do all the work.

"The saga of my eyes changed my career path, as well as my personal life. I needed new areas to work in and could no longer be a secretary. In having to alter the way I used my vision and my brain, I began to see the world much differently. My eyes deepened my interest in holistic healing, spiritual values, and metaphysics. I became intrigued with the book

Egyptian Mysteries by Lucy Lamy and its discussion on the myth of the Eye of Horus."

This Eye symbolizes the devine light imprisoned in matter which must be liberated. Thus, it is said that the Eye is the seat of the soul and is all-powerful, for it possesses in itself the means for this deliverance. Through the crossing of the nerve fibers in the optic chiasma, the left half of the brain sees with the right eye and the right half with the left eye. The interweaving of perceptions renders us conscious of objects and their forms. Thus, the Eye is related in Egyptian thought to the divinities of weaving, to sia, knowledge, and to Sia, the divinity of knowledge, whose name is written hieroglyphically as a piece of cloth, because the eye, our predominant means of gaining knowledge, shares the principle of crossing by which a fabric is made.

Kathleen had to grow new eyes due to an accident of nature. Most of us, however, prefer a figurative regrowth to a literal one. This is something we can all do.

How to Grow New Eyes

THERE ARE TWO WAYS to reframe your own circumstances and grow new eyes. One is by the accidental method which results in the "ah ha" examples of Wayne Dyer, Jimmy/Jay, and myself. The second is to do it purposely. We are powerful human beings with a strong ability to force change in our perceptions. When we are in a situation which is clearly not making us feel competent, confident, or in control, then we must have the chutzpah to grow new eyes and reframe our perception of that situation. We must get ourselves into a receptive mood. We must find a place to quietly relax and use a form of meditation to clear the fog from our minds. If Zen-style meditation is not your thing, then a quiet moment in the bathtub, the hot tub, your favorite chair or corner of the room will do. You must not be distracted by anything else. (Make sure you are not doing this while driving a car in heavy traffic.)

The next step is to smile broadly, which forces the brain to be more positive. We then visualize the new perception, which can be as absurd as we wish it to be. Once we have reframed the picture of our circumstance, we must state the reframed notion loudly and clearly. Apparently, our brain is quite in tune to our own voices, so what we say out loud serves to reinforce our new perceptions. Here are two examples:

You are facing a health crisis. You are fearful. You must relax, visualize the challenge (not problem) that your body and mind are facing and further visualize your return to health. You say out loud, "I am strong, I am healthy, I am grateful for the good things in my life and for the medical care I will be receiving. I will focus on how good it feels when my health starts to return, and I will be forever grateful for every healthy day I have yet to live." Are you feeling better already? Of course you are. You have now regained control over a very serious situation which could drag you down if you did not reframe it and grow new eyes.

Here's another example. Your marriage is a mess. You and your spouse are not communicating, and you suspect infidelity. With your old eyes, you feel angry, jealous, scared and insecure. But with great chutzpah, you reframe the situation and speak of it in another way. "This is a troubling time for our marriage, but I am positive that the outcome will be right. I am strong and loving and willing to face the challenges of this marriage. Whatever way it turns out, I am a whole person – valuable, attractive and strong."

While these two examples apply to an individual's personal life, it is equally important to grow new eyes in one's professional life. One of my favorite stories is about the barber in the small town who was rattled when he learned of the mass-market haircutting company moving to a shop near his. He feared he would lose customers to the cheaper competitor. He hired a marketing consultant who had great chutzpah. Next to the sign where the competitor advertised its $8 haircuts, our barber friend put up a large sign which said, "We *fix* $8 haircuts."

We all smile when we think of the confidence and gall of the barber who put out his own competitive sign. Reframing is something we can all do.

"The real voyage of discovery consists not in
seeking new landscapes, but in having new eyes."
— MARCEL PROUST

Trait #8

Count
Your
Blessings

"Success is getting what you want;
happiness is wanting what you get."

When times are tough, we must make a conscious decision to focus on what is right, not on what is wrong. In order to have more chutzpah, we must, therefore, count our blessings – and keep on counting. Is the glass half empty as the pessimist sees it, or is it half full as the optimist sees it? Either way you have the same amount to drink, but your perspective makes all the difference. It is an unfortunate fact that sometimes we forget how much we have and what our blessings are until we no longer have them. Let me tell you the story of Mary Ann.

Mary Ann

MARY ANN WAS BORN into a wonderful, loving family in a traditional American neighborhood. She had a great education and traveled the world. She was bright, beautiful, and articulate. And boy, could she talk. Talking was one of the things she did best. She had a quick mind and a quicker tongue, and thinking on her feet was one of her best talents. Then one day something happened to change all that.

In January of 1993, Mary Ann and her husband were involved in a terrible auto accident. The last thing she remembers is reading a book while her husband drove, and the next thing she remembers is waking up in a hospital five weeks later. Due to the heroic efforts of an off-duty fireman, she was rescued from the car and flown by helicopter to the hospital just in time for the brain surgery which saved her life. Her neurosurgeon said she was minutes away from death, and he was worried that she might be in a "persistent vegetative state." A second surgery was needed to quell the swelling of her brain and keep it from oozing out of the hole on the left side of her head.

You may be surprised to learn, as I was, that a person doesn't just "come to" from being in a coma. It is a very slow awakening and, for most of the time, the patient's friends, family, and physicians do not know the extent of the injury or the possibility of recovery. Mary Ann's family and friends waited anxiously for any signs of consciousness, and slowly some were evident. But the right side of her body was paralyzed. She needed help sitting up, eating, walking, showering, and going to the bathroom — and she couldn't speak. For months she endured painful physical therapy and frustrating speech therapy. Everything was coming back, slowly but surely, except for her speech. The doctors call it "expressive aphasia," which comes from losing certain cells in the brain and needing to find alternate channels to turn thoughts into words. Mary Ann can now think and write in the same way she did before the accident, but finding words, particularly in stressful situations, is difficult.

Mary Ann could have felt sorry for herself, concentrating on all the things she can no longer do. Her balance is not as good as it was before the accident and her movements are much slower. Her hair is shorter and is taking a long time to regrow after being shaved off several times for her surgeries. For many months, she had to wear a helmet on her head, even in public, to protect her fragile skull. She lost her job as the Downtown Redevelopment Director for the city, a job she had trained many years for and in which she had already accomplished a great deal. She was placed in a position requiring less public speaking and confrontation.

But Mary Ann does not like to focus on what she cannot do now, nor do as well as before her accident. In fact, Mary Ann prefers to tell people what she can now do *better* than she did before.

Mary Ann has really learned to listen. Now that she cannot speak at full speed, she says she must listen more. A whole new world has opened up to her as she has learned to listen to her friends, her family, and her coworkers. She learned to listen with her ears, her eyes, and her heart, And she learned through looking and listening what love really means. Love is the commitment of her friends and family who visited her every day and took care of her many physical and emotional needs. Love is the devotion of a husband who showered with her in the hospital so the nurses wouldn't have to do it.

Mary Ann considers herself blessed, and counts her blessings every day. "Happiness is being near people you love" was one of the things she wrote on her notepad when she could not speak at all. "Each day should be unwrapped like a precious gift" is her final entry. For Mary Ann, if every day wasn't special enough before, it certainly is now.

Counting her blessings is something Mary Ann does over and over again. With great chutzpah, she is speaking to audiences about her experiences, hoping to inspire others to continue on and to count their blessings as well. She is becoming a motivational speaker, addressing other brain-injured people, as well as general audiences, who are awed by her courage and her commitment. We can all learn from that courage and positive attitude. If we focus on our blessings every day, we will be able to move forward, achieve our dreams, and reach the ultimate in our success.

We all know that counting blessings is difficult when things feel all wrong. When we endure tragic events, lose loved ones, our jobs, our homes, and, seemingly, our dreams, it is easier to enumerate what we have lost. It takes a great deal of chutzpah to count, instead, all that we have. And I know. I have been there myself.

It was a very rough year before my 45th birthday. The country's economic recession had taken its toll on me and my business. Again, I felt like I was struggling just to maintain. My income dropped, my health suffered, and several of my friends and family members died. There seemed only darkness, no light. But then I remembered something my mother told me when I was growing up. "If you hang all your dirty laundry out the window (she knows of this because she was brought up in the tenements in New York), and everybody else puts their dirty laundry out as well, you will soon pull yours back in shame because it is so much less than everyone else's." I had to smile. Once again, the sage remarks of my mother gave me a new view of things.

So I sat down at my desk and I wrote out "45 Things I am Thankful for on My 45th Birthday." I include them here for you, although some of them are very personal. They are in no particular order, but how they came to me. At first, I thought I would never be able to reach the number 45. But with a little imagination, some positive introspection, and a great deal of chutzpah, I achieved a complete list.

1. John (my son)
2. Mom and Dad
3. My other relatives
4. My close friends
5. My good health
6. My house
7. My cars
8. My colleagues
9. My drive, persistence
10. My sense of humor
11. My cats
12. The memory of my dogs
13. My books
14. My jewelry
15. My clothes
16. My community involvements
17. Cable TV
18. TV in my room
19. Working at home
20. My work relations
21. My flexibility, creativity
22. My condo in LV
23. "Peep" my bird
24. My exercise club
25. My love of reading
26. My ability to dance
27. My artwork
28. My advisors
29. RAB-my mentor
30. John's friends
31. My uncles
32. Diet bars
33. My repairman
34. The Nail Ladies
35. Crossword puzzles
36. Espresso latté
37. My sexual self
38. Lovers – past, present, and future
39. Big John & Gargo (my ex & his wife – really!)
40. My front yard
41. My love of language
42. My education & degrees
43. My ability to speak in public
44. My naps
45. My future

By the time I finished, I was feeling great. In fact, I was feeling a little guilty to be so blessed! And I was finally able to move forward.

I challenge you to do the same. Make a list of all your blessings and have the number equal your age in years. Then every year on your birthday, add to the list. Of course, if you need more room, attach additional sheets!

12

Trait #9

Laugh at Life

*"If at first you do succeed,
it's probably your father's business."*

Throughout my career as a public speaker,
I've had many opportunities to embarrass myself and to react
with humor to maintain my dignity and poise.

Not long ago, I was addressing a large group of medical
group administrators. I had just begun my presentation, and
what I was attempting to say to them was, "First, you have to
start with . ." Instead, what came out of my mouth was, "First,
you have to fart."

I could not believe what had just happened! I had never in
my life said that word publicly, and I certainly had not intended to do so that day.

Now in these types of situations, a professional speaker is
trained to continue speaking as if nothing has happened, so as
not to draw attention to the flub. The thought of doing just
that crossed my mind. But then I looked at the audience. And
they were no longer looking at me. In fact, they were looking
everywhere but at me. They were looking down, they were
looking around, they were poking one another in the ribs and

giving one another sidelong looks.

It was obvious that not only had they heard what I had said *very* clearly, but *they* knew that *I* knew that *they* knew it was a big mistake. I briefly considered the possibility of continuing on as if nothing had happened, but I knew if I did, my audience would be uncomfortably out of control the rest of the day, just trying to hold back their laughter.

I could have continued being embarrassed. I *should* have been embarrassed. But instead, I chose another approach. With great chutzpah, I looked directly at the audience, paused for a moment and then said, "Well, it is true. Sometimes you just have to fart." And it brought down the house.

The barely repressed titters of laughter gave way to gales and howls. Tears were running down the faces of these professional, and normally reserved, men and women. My audience members held their sides and let all the tension of the moment come out in their guffaws. When the laughter finally subsided, and they were starting to regain their composure, I added, "You should consider yourselves lucky. At least I just *said* the word."

Humor

HUMOR. THAT'S WHAT I USED to get me through this potentially embarrassing situation, and am I glad I did. Which leads me to the discussion of the next important trait necessary for more chutzpah – that of developing and using humor. We need to look at the world in a funny way and laugh our way to success. Granted, there are many situations in this life which are not very funny. Yet that is precisely why we must learn to see the humor at these times in order to be better armed to face them. Humor is a natural coping mechanism which can help make tolerable those things which are most bleak or unpleasant, at least for the moment. We all need to find ways to laugh through our tears and rejoice in the miracle of humor.

Laughter and humor are indeed wondrous things with miraculous powers. What other medium has the ability to immediately break down barriers between complete strangers.

"Laughing together banishes loneliness and isolation, creates social bonds even as it recognizes differences." – HUGH DUNCAN

Humor facilitates communication and has the magical ability to shorten the emotional distance between two people. People who laugh at the same thing find an instant bond and rapport. Laughter puts us on an equal footing with others and puts them at ease. Laughter relieves stress and anger, reduces tension, and serves as an emotional cathartic release.

Humor is often beneficial in establishing or maintaining our relationships. Couples in long-term successful marriages often report that laughing together helps hold them together.

Mirth is valuable in the workplace as well. So much so, in fact, that many corporations send their serious-about-themselves executives to intensive humor workshops to awaken their funny bones. The hope is that these executives will then return to their businesses and use appropriate humor to motivate their workers, stimulate their creativity and de-stress the work environment.

Not only is laughter good for the mind and spirit, it is good for you physically. Laughter's effect on the human body actually resembles exercise in many ways. It triggers the release of endorphins. The actual act of laughing involves the respiratory, cardiovascular, muscular, endocrine and central nervous systems. Afterward, these physiological measurements sink below their previous level – so the harder we laugh, the greater they fall afterward. The end result is that we feel relaxed. Think about the last time you had a good old-fashioned belly laugh. Didn't you feel great afterward?

Laughing Through the Pain

THE CURATIVE POWER OF LAUGHTER in overcoming illness has long been recognized. Perhaps one of the most well-known stories of an individual using mirth to stave off a life-threatening illness is that of Norman Cousins. Cousins was the editor of the *Saturday Review* in New York City. In 1964, he was stricken with a painful, debilitating and usually fatal disease called ankylosing spondylitis, an illness which progressively degenerates the body's connective tissue, including the spine.

His doctors told him that he had a one in 500 chance of surviving the disease. In essence, Norman Cousins was given a death sentence. But he was a bright, chutzy man. He decided to risk abandoning the treatment offered by modern medicine – hospitalization, pain medication and sleeping pills – and instead took steps to cure himself. And in doing so, he revolutionized the view held in the field of medicine today regarding the mind-body connection.

First, he decided to inject himself with massive doses of vitamin C. In those days, vitamin C was being touted as having curative powers for the common cold, but not for anything as serious as ankylosing spondylitis. However, it was Cousins' belief that the ascorbic acid would strengthen his body's connective tissues.

Next, he decided to change the negative way in which his disease was being viewed by determinedly talking to himself in positive terms and by visualizing his own healing.

Finally, Cousins decided that he needed humor to heal himself, and so he began watching old Marx Brothers films to induce laughter. Cousins discovered that 10 minutes of genuine belly laughter had an analgesic effect and would give him at least two hours of pain-free sleep. So laugh, laugh, laugh he did. In fact, he was laughing so hard – and annoying the other sick patients in the hospital – that he checked himself out of the hospital and into the Waldorf Astoria Hotel (thereby probably saving himself several hundred dollars a day).

Soon he was off the morphine, and almost immediately the sedimentation rate in his blood went down, which also meant his infection rate was decreasing. Within just a couple of months, he was up and out of bed. One year after being told by his doctors that his chance of survival was virtually nil, Norman Cousins was on his feet again, practically pain-free and playing the piano. He had literally laughed himself to health. But his story doesn't end there.

Cousins returned to his job at the *Saturday Review,* but was a changed man, having faced down a potentially fatal disease. A great deal of chutzpah was now coursing through his veins, and he knew he had something more to accomplish with his life. So, along with a large monetary grant from Mrs. Ray Croc, widow of the founder of McDonald's restaurants, Cousins opened up the Department of Psychoneuroimmunology at UCLA Medical Center. This department was established to study one thing – the effect of positive emotions on the health and healing of the human body. For a person not trained in the medical sciences, this was certainly a chutzy thing to do! And now he had the credibility to make others listen to him.

In the last couple of years before his death, Cousins' faculty had actually developed a way to study positive emotions and their effect on the body. Cousins died at the age of 75 from a massive heart attack. But by taking control of his own life at a time when he was given little hope, he not only increased his own life expectancy by an additional 30 years, but also changed all of our lives for the better.

Humor Diffuses an Embarrassing Situation

SUCCESSFUL, CHUTZY PEOPLE find ways to use humor to get through life's toughest challenges. Probably my favorite story is about my friend's mother, Mary, and the way in which she used humor to put her doctor at ease during an embarrassing medical procedure.

Mary was only in her late 40's when she was diagnosed with uterine cancer. Her treatment necessitated the insertion of cobalt cones into her body, and the doctor who was giving her these treatments happened to be a young new intern. So there was Mary in that God-awful position that only women can relate to, with her feet up in stirrups, while the intern proceeded to try to insert cones inside her for treatment. He was very nervous and embarrassed. The first one was too big. He tried a smaller one. All the while his hands were shaking, but he was finally able to get the smaller cone inserted. As he accomplished his task, he looked at Mary and said, "There, I got it."

Mary peered around her sheet-shrouded knees, looked the young, nervous intern in the eye and said, "You know, young man, if you would have just kissed me first, the big one would have fit."

Gallows Humor

DIFFERENT TYPES OF HUMOR are used to help us survive terrible situations and to move on to higher levels of existence. Gallows humor – or black humor – has been used for centuries by people enduring the worst conditions and situations. These people, like survivors of the Nazi concentration camps, found that sick, black, perverted humor was sometimes their only lifeline. When they relate something they laughed at while they were imprisoned, the rest of us, of course, don't get the humor of it. They often respond, "Well, I guess you just had to be there!"

Self-Deprecating Humor

SELF-DEPRECATING HUMOR is also a valuable success tool which takes a great deal of chutzpah to use, whether in making light of our own selves or in handling others' uncharitable opinions of us. Some well-known quotes illustrate how famous individuals used self-deprecating humor. Abraham Lincoln said, "Some people say that I'm two-faced. Now, how could that possibly be true? If I had two faces, would I have picked this one?" Before being operated on after the assassination attempt made on his life, former president Reagan said, "I sure hope the surgeons are Republicans." And Henry Kissinger once said, "The nice thing about being a celebrity is that *now* when you bore people, they think it's *their* fault."

Being able to poke fun at ourselves shows others that we are human, that we are completely comfortable with who we are, and that we have enough confidence in our own abilities to make fun of our foibles. If we take ourselves too seriously, we lose an important edge. And if we do not laugh at ourselves, others probably will.

It takes great chutzpah to see the world as funny, particularly when it doesn't seem very funny at all. But humor is a very important tool. Whether we laugh at our situation or ourselves, we get to our next level when we find humor.

"I believe that imagination is stronger than knowledge.
That myth is more potent than history.
That dreams are more powerful than facts.
That hope always triumphs over experience.
That laughter is the only cure for grief.
And I believe that love is stronger than death."

— ROBERT FULGHUM
All I Really Need to Know, I Learned in Kindergarten

13

Trait #10

Love Yourself and Honor Your Roots

"Everybody's a self-made man, but only the successful are willing to admit it."

In order to be truly successful we need to love ourselves. Not just *like,* but *love.* Successful people have learned to accept themselves as they are, to love themselves unconditionally, and to pass that love on to everyone else with whom they come into contact. However, learning to love one's self is not always an easy task. Certain childhood experiences misshape our perceptions of ourselves and have a profound effect on the development of a very necessary, healthy self-esteem. This was certainly the situation in Joe's early life.

Joe

JOE ALWAYS KNEW he was a "somebody," but his father thought otherwise. Joe was the runt in his family, small in stature and frail in health during a time in the Italian-American immigrant family history when male size and looks were considered a family's "asset." One day he overheard his father say to his mother, "You know, Joe is a dandelion in a bed of roses." Joe was both hurt and angry. He was the smallest boy in a family of 9 children, 7 boys and 2 girls. His father was a proud, stern, Old World, blue-collar worker living on the outskirts of Chicago, who took pride in his big, strapping, good-looking sons...and then there was Joe.

Joe was trying to learn to love himself, but the unkind words of his father echoed in his soul for years to come. In those days, the "fight game" was topped by Italian boxers like Marciano and Graziano. Joe hoped to get his father's recognition by fighting or, more accurately, scrapping. He would pick fights with other kids just to be recognized and get some attention. But it wasn't working for Joe in the way he expected. So in his pain and knowing he had something of value to share, Joe turned to humor to reach out. He found that he could win the admiration of his peers and family members by being comedic. For him, the word *comedic* became *co - medic*, as it helped heal his feelings of frustration to become the terrific human being he is today.

Joe became a nightclub comedy entertainer during his stint in the Army in Europe. He traveled around Europe and England trying to make a name for himself, taking any gig that came his way with the courage of the scrapper he always was. One night he was sent to do a schtick at a working man's Irish pub. The setting was typical of nightclubs, but even more so. The stench of unwashed bodies permeated the room as a cloud of cigar and cigarette smoke hung over it. The men in the bar were rather large, burley, and outspoken. As he was introduced and started his routine, they were yelling and talking, and Joe could not even be heard. After a few minutes, Joe realized he had lost the audience (indeed, he had never found them) and bolted toward the side of the stage to escape. As he reached the wings, the pub manager stopped him abruptly. "Young man," he said, "I will not pay you a dime unless you go out there and finish your routine."

Joe needed the money, for the trip to this pub had taken every cent he had. He had no choice. Joe faced his fears, spun around on his heel, and marched back out to the center of the stage. This time, however, instead of standing, he plopped down on the edge of the stage, crossed his legs, leaned forward, and whispered to the crowd. "Listen, you guys. I don't have a cent in my pocket, and if I don't finish this routine, I won't have money to get home. So if you will just calm down for a few minutes and listen to what I have to say, we all might have a good time." The crowd, unaccustomed to whispers and soft language, quieted down just like the people in that old Merrill Lynch commercial. With their startled looks for encouragement, Joe launched into his routine, and they all had a terrific time. One man in the back even yelled to the others, "Shut up, you guys. Let him talk. He's funny."

It had taken a great deal of chutzpah for Joe to go back on stage and face a rude, inattentive crowd that night. But Joe had once again learned one of the lessons in his life – humor is a universal language and can heal across borders. Joe was certainly learning to appreciate himself, to respect his talent, and to look for broader markets.

The dandelion was transforming itself into a beautiful rose, with many layers and great promise. Joe then moved himself from comedy routines to working with corporations. He feels his job is to help people jump-start their lives.

"So many people have given up and are not aware that they are so much more valuable than they think they are. We are all greater than we think we are. We all have many songs yet unsung and it is my job to help people get in touch with their songs."

In addition to working with corporations, Joe also works

with at-risk children, although he hates that label. He helps kids get in touch with their inner beauty, their talents, and their natural instincts to help them become more of what they can really be. His newest program is entitled, "Putting the Human Back Into Being." His challenge is to help people surpass self-imposed limitations by learning to love and trust themselves as he, himself, has learned to do. His advice to all of us is, "Don't listen to other people. They are usually wrong. If it feels right for you, just do it!"

Joe is truly an inspiration, as he helps put the *human* back into *being*. He no longer looks or acts like a dandelion, but more like a beautiful bouquet of spring flowers, blending the softest aromas with the brightest of petals. He reminds us all that we are beautiful on the inside and that we must love ourselves, for loving ourself is the first step towards true achievement and success.

So why is self-love so difficult? For one reason, the effects of negative experiences in our early childhood can linger throughout our adult lives. Doreen tells her story.

Doreen

ONE SUNDAY AFTERNOON when she was about nine years old, Doreen was on her driveway practicing with a new top. This top had a string around the bottom and had to be held and thrown just so, with a certain speed and angle, to allow it to spin on its metal point. Doreen was not the most coordinated child, but she was working hard by herself to get the throw right. Her father, who had been working nearby in the yard, became frustrated with Doreen's lack of progress and decided to help her. He was a rather gruff man and the more he insisted Doreen do it *his* way, the more intimidated Doreen felt. "Every time the top fell over," she said, "so did my self-esteem. The more my father yelled at me, the harder it was to do any part correctly. Before I knew it, there was a crowd of family members and neighbors watching the debacle. I was humiliated, but my father decided to persevere anyway. The more he yelled, the worst it got. Finally, I threw the thing down and went sobbing into the house to bury my head under my pillow. The public humiliation was terrible and for that moment I hated my dad. The top wouldn't balance and neither would I."

Doreen says it took years for her to rebuild her self-esteem, piece-by-piece. Luckily, she was always good in academics and through her studies achieved recognition and appreciation. She graduated with scholarships from high school and cum laude from college. She is now a psychologist who helps people improve their self-esteem. "Feelings of inadequacy are a daily demon," she says. "I know that is true for myself and for many other people. If I can help others fight that demon and achieve small successes in their lives, then, indeed, I also am a success."

So what happens if you do not have good self-esteem? People who do not love themselves do not feel worthy of success. They are fearful of taking new steps, asserting themselves, and getting what they need and want. People with low self-esteem find it difficult to face life's problems without feeling smothered by them. They avoid new situations and challenging opportunities in order to protect their fragile self-concept. It then becomes a self-fulfilling prophecy. These people do not challenge themselves and, therefore, have fewer successes. The lack of success, in turn, contributes to their feelings of low self-esteem. An unhealthy psychological cycle is perpetuated.

On the other hand, if we have confidence in our self-worth, and feel secure within ourselves, we not only seek new challenges and opportunities, but relish them. Another new cycle is created, but a much healthier one. People who feel good about themselves take on more challenges, responsibilities, and higher-level opportunities. With success, they feel even better about themselves and seek more opportunities. High self-esteem people – chutzy people – dream of lofty goals and take the necessary risks to achieve them. Low self-esteem people seek to remain in their comfort (or dis-comfort) zone to search for a security which never really exists.

People with high self-esteem are able to handle setbacks and obstacles more smoothly because they are able to differentiate their selves from their problems. Low self-esteem people believe that their problems *are* themselves.

People with healthy self-love are open, honest, and direct and thereby have open and honest relationships. They have close families and friends, and enjoy deep levels of intimacy within all their rich relationships. These people also have good relationships in their work and professional lives, and tend to command the respect of coworkers, subordinates, and bosses. People with low self-esteem do not have the confidence to be open, honest, and direct in their relationships. They often suffer from loneliness and isolation due to their indirect and sometimes hostile communications. Their personal relationships are limited, as are their relationships in the workplace. Some overachieving people with low self-esteem are often workaholics who get some feeling of success from work achievements, but little from relationships. But even workaholics limit their success due to lack of balance. As we have discussed in prior chapters, in order to be truly successful, one must balance all aspects of one's life, including the physical, psychological, social, emotional, and spiritual needs.

People who feel lovable are able to love others. People who feel unlovable cannot. People who feel lovable, likewise, know who they are and expect and receive good treatment from everyone else. People who do not feel lovable often allow others to abuse, embarrass, and humiliate them. Obviously, people cannot be truly successful while allowing others to mistreat them. High self-esteem people dance in such a way that their partners are equal, sturdy, and respectful. Low self-esteem people dance with partners who are also of low self-esteem and who may be either submissive or aggressive. A successful dance, where partners float across the ballroom floor with grace, elegance, and in sync with the music, is a beautiful sight. However, a dance with partners stepping on one another's feet is clumsy, awkward, and even pitiful. It is obvious that successful people dance like the first couple and, in fact, can glide gracefully on the ballroom floor of life – even by themselves. Such is chutzpah!

How Self-Esteem Can Be Injured

FROM BOTH Joe's and Doreen's stories, we see the impact parents have on the development of their children's self-esteem. Parents who themselves lack healthy self-esteem can injure the budding self-esteem of their children by cruel, thoughtless remarks, inappropriate punishment, and even inattention. Remember the esteem problems of Jimmy/Jay stemming from his mother's aloofness. Children are both delicate and resilient. They can be easily injured by an untoward remark or a debasing comment, but will also seek opportunities for self-enhancement. Joe scrapped himself to a high level of self-esteem by using humor. Doreen fights her demons daily by helping others with theirs.

Even accomplished professional people sometimes have trouble with self-esteem. A study a few years ago on the "Impostor Syndrome" suggested that many professional people feel they are really inadequate. Many such professionals cover up their inadequacy by working hard and achieving at new levels. What a sad commentary! How delicate must our frail egos be that we make self-love conditional on achievement – and even then have doubts.

How to Improve Self-Esteem

1. Celebrate Your Uniqueness

There are a number of ways to learn to love yourself, accept yourself, and be more successful. First of all, you must celebrate your uniqueness. We are all unique and beautiful in our own way. The fact of our creation is a miracle in and of itself. Celebrating your uniqueness means identifying your strengths and talents and working them to the best advantage. Each one of us has a special gift. Identifying that gift is the first step toward self-love and esteem. If we feel there are areas of inadequacy or ugliness, then we must remember this is only in the eye of the beholder. We can certainly learn to accept them – every pimple, wrinkle, or extra ounce of fat – and love ourselves for the unique creation we are. I, for one, never intend to apologize for taking any space on this earth and I do not expect you to either.

2. Become Your Own Best Friend

The second way to improve self-esteem is to become your own best friend. We cannot always count on the kindnesses of others to help us feel better about ourselves. If we treat ourselves in the kind, considerate way that our best friends do, then we can strengthen our esteem. How would your best friend handle your expression of self-debasement? Wouldn't he or she listen intently, disagree hotly, and then tell you that you are special, loved, and needed? Do that for yourself.

Wouldn't your best friend be available to take you to lunch or shopping or on a boating trip to help you with your sadness or disappointment? You can certainly do that for yourself. Wouldn't your best friend make you laugh at your dire situation and help you see yourself and the world as funny? Do that for yourself, also. Whatever your best friend would do to you, and for you, to make you feel better about yourself, you can do for yourself. My friends are always good, nonjudgmental listeners, who help me laugh through troubled times. I know I can count on them, but I also know I can count on myself.

3. Befriend Someone Else

The third way to improve your self-esteem is to become a best friend to someone else. Giving to others makes you feel better about yourself. Joe helps at-risk children and serious-minded corporate executives. Doreen helps low-esteem women reenter the work force with feelings of confidence. If you give to others and accomplish a good deed every day, you will find a slow, but steady, improvement in your self-esteem. Everyone should do this. No matter how good we feel about ourselves, we should do a daily good deed. In the chapter on "Give and Give Back," I tell the stories of Eugene Lange and Ondra Berry. These are people who give and give back. They do it because they are grateful for their own successes and want to contribute to the success of others. A very important by-product, however, is their own feeling of heightened self-worth.

4. Accomplish Something

The next way to improve self-esteem is to accomplish something, even something small. Nothing quite succeeds like success. The largest project in our lives, whether professional or personal, can seem overwhelming at first. But once we slice the large salami project into thin, manageable slices, we are able to make headway. Even tiny steps forward give a feeling of accomplishment. Many people with low self-esteem tend to procrastinate. They put off projects because they lack confidence. The cycle is evident again. Procrastination breeds feelings of worthlessness, which feeds feelings of low self-esteem, which causes further procrastination. In order to break this cycle, you must start with a small successful step. For two years, I procrastinated writing this book. In some ways, I felt unworthy to write a book on success because of my own struggles. So I made a deal with myself. I planned the project and broke it into the tiniest pieces possible and started with the first one. I told myself that I only had to work one hour. Sitting down to start was the second hardest part. Stopping, once I got started, was the first hardest part. For, you see, nothing feels as good as success. As I saw my ideas emerge into shape on an empty page, I felt my confidence growing. I was eager to proceed and have worked steadily on the book since.

> *"Mañana is the busiest day of the week."*
> – SPANISH PROVERB

5. Stand for Something Positive

Another step to improving self-esteem is to stand for something positive. Know who you are and what your values are, and stand for them mightily. People who stand for nothing will fall for anything. What do you stand for? What are you willing to fight for and, indeed, in some instances, die for? To the extent that your values are positive and affirming of the worthiness of life, you will enjoy a feeling of great self-worth. Kathleen certainly boosted her self-esteem when she found the chutzpah to face Congress and testify to the need to legalize certain drugs for use by terminal patients, including her dying, suffering father. Mary Ann helps her sometimes faltering self-esteem by talking to other brain-damaged people and encouraging them to count their blessings. Valerie stands for health and balance, and boosts her self-esteem when she talks to others about her struggles with anorexia. Marie faces her daily demons when she helps others deal with the pain of sexual abuse. These people each stand for something positive, celebrate their uniquenesses, and feel good about themselves.

6. **Enjoy the Success of Others**

    Another important way to improve self-esteem is to truly enjoy the success of others. People with low self-esteem feel diminished by the success of others in a negative, competitive way. They feel jealous and envious of the good life of others, and can actually make themselves sick by comparing themselves unfavorably and wishing others had less. It is interesting to note that in the Ten Commandments, there is one commandment which outlaws "coveting thy neighbor's wife." Not only is coveting others not good for society, it is not good for one's self-esteem. People with good self-esteem can enjoy the success of others while feeling occasional pangs of jealousy. A friend of mine recently inherited a great deal of money, enough so she will never have to work again in her lifetime. A small part of me was envious of her new-found wealth and freedom, but a bigger part of me was absolutely delighted for her. In fact, I basked in her joy with her. I told her I wanted to know everything she was doing with the money and how it affected her life so that I could have those positive feelings with her. I am truly happy about her new fortune and the opportunities it presents for her. I also know she has struggled in her life and has earned every one of those opportunities and the new-found freedom. In a way, I am enjoying her good fortune almost as much as she is!

7. **Be Assertive**

The next step in improving your self-esteem is to learn to express yourself assertively. Assertive expression is neither submissive nor aggressive. It is open, honest, and direct, and it builds solid relationships. The more we are able to express our needs, desires, and concerns, the more competent we are in getting all we want in life. Isn't the true measure of success the ability to live our lives as we wish? There are a number of books and courses to help you learn how to express yourself more directly and clearly. Please avail yourself of these opportunities. You will find a whole new world of joy opening up from your ability to better express yourself. Part of honest communication also involves how you handle your errors, mistakes, and faux pas.

8. **Admit Your Mistakes – Loudly!**

The next important step in improving your self-esteem is how you admit your mistakes. We all make mistakes. "To err is human, to forgive [ourselves] is divine." People with low self-esteem tend to blame others, deny culpability, and shove mistakes under the proverbial rug. People with high self-esteem, however, admit their mistakes loudly and clearly. After Judge Mills Lane erred in how he handled a case as a deputy district attorney, he learned that he was going to get a private censure. He got on the phone and into their faces: "If I have done something wrong, then I deserve a *public* censure, not a private one. In this case I deserve it. I made a big mistake and I owe it to the people of this county to admit it loudly and clearly. I want this made public and I want it opened right now. I do not want to hear about it three years later." What great chutzpah it took for Mills Lane to turn a private censure into a public one. This is one guy who will never suffer from low self-esteem!

I was proud of myself because of the way I handled my speaking faux pas described in the chapter on humor. I could have glossed over it and pretended it didn't happen, but instead I faced it, addressed it, and was able to move on. My self-esteem must have been at a high point that day.

We all admire people who accept blame for their mistakes much more so than people who deny it or blame others. An article in *Time Magazine,* May 8, 1995, describes, "How to Apologize Just Like the Pros." With tongue-in-cheek, they offer the following advice: If you have insulted someone: 1) Suggest the problem lies not in what you said, but in how others reacted to it. 2) Explain that your cruel remarks were actually all in good fun. This is what Howard Stern, who suffers from over-chutzpah, said to justify ridiculing Hispanic music in general and slain diva Selena in particular. 3) Assure the people you've insulted that actually you think they're just swell. 4) Blame it on some mysterious physical or mental tic. 5) Finally, blame it on the media. The over-chutzpahed U. S. Senator Jesse Helms said, "In an informal telephone interview with a local reporter, I made an off-hand remark. Of course, I did not expect it to be taken literally." He said this about his suggestion that Bill Clinton would need a bodyguard if visiting North Carolina military bases.

So we all make mistakes. But we can enhance our self-esteem if we admit them openly and loudly and then move on. Do not let the fear of making mistakes keep you from accomplishing your goals and being successful. It is easier to get forgiveness than permission. This is the chutzpah connection.

9. Invest In Yourself

A final way to improve one's self-esteem is to make steady and positive investments in yourself. You must honor yourself and take good care of yourself. The food you eat, the clothing you wear, the books you read, the movies you watch, the people you relate to and the education you acquire should all be positive. If you eat well, exercise appropriately, rest, keep an open mind, and learn-learn-learn, then you will be investing in a valuable commodity – yourself. To love yourself more, you must do good things for yourself. Doing good things will, in turn, make you feel better about yourself. Start today. Eliminate habits which are hurtful: stop smoking, reduce your alcohol intake, eat a healthier diet, take a walk around the block, read a good book, listen to beautiful music, take your kids to the park, and enjoy all that life has to offer. This time you spend with yourself is an investment toward your own success.

Exceed Yourself

Once you have learned to love yourself and accept yourself as you are, then you can take steps to exceed yourself. Psychologist Carl Rogers said, "The curious paradox is that when I accept myself as I am, then I can change." It is indeed an interesting paradox. We must accept ourselves as we are and then take steps to exceed ourselves. To be successful in life, we should not compete with others, only with ourselves. As Joe says, "We are capable of a whole lot more than we know we are." Tom Kubistant learned that lesson in his life.

Tom

TOM WAS A SHY, BRIGHT, introverted young man, whose father worked in manufacturing and whose mother stayed home with the family. Tom had a normal, healthy upbringing and was taught by his father to be independent, resourceful, and practical. It was during high school, and those very troubling teen years, that Tom developed cystic acne, a disfiguring facial problem. As the pustules grew on his face, he turned his feelings inward. Not particularly outgoing, Tom became more reclusive, both emotionally and socially.

Tom's father wanted him to do something practical with his life, such as becoming a watchmaker. But Tom was more interested in understanding people than in understanding mechanical things. His high school and college years were unremarkable. He was graduated from the university with a "C" average. Miraculously, he got into graduate school and earned a doctorate in education. He wanted a life easier than his father's, using an education instead of a strong back.

Tom had a strong back, but not strong knees. In 1972, he had major surgery on his left knee. The damage was so extensive that the physician told Tom he might never walk again, or if he did, to count on having a limp. What a blow to this young man who was quite athletic and who performed so well on the tennis court, the track, and the golf course. Physical challenges and accomplishments were his outlet for deep emotions and he worried about what he would be able to do now. Part of the healing process from the knee surgery involved physical therapy. The doctor told him he would be able to go only so far with the weights and repetitions, and that he should not try to pass those marks, as it could cause further injury to his knee, probably crippling him forever.

But like so many of our other chutzy heroes, Tom was somewhat of a rebel. When he got to the point in the weight regimen where the physician told him he should stop, he decided to go beyond. With persistence, pain, and determination he forged forward. Several times a day he exercised his leg and watched it grow in size and strength. It became his raison d'etre. Soon his bad knee grew stronger than his good knee, so he had to exercise that one also.

As Tom's knee became rehabilitated, so did his mind. In putting the strength back into his knee and being able to walk normally again, he learned of the fallacy in the term *limitation*. With his own style and chutzpah, he redefined the word limitation to mean frontier. Tom wrote a book which came from his experience and from the new eyes he grew in rehabilitating his body and his mind.

Performing Your Best is a guide to psychological skills for high achievers. Dr. Tom Kubistant is one of the country's most popular and versatile speakers. He owns a training and consulting firm that works with athletes, performing artists, and businesspeople. In "walking his talk" every day, he doesn't falter and he doesn't limp. He helps others find the courage to face life's challenges by viewing them never as limitations, but only as frontiers.

We should all heed Tom's message. Limitations are usually self-imposed. To be truly successful, we must seek ways to go beyond. In the chapter on growing new eyes, we learned the importance of reframing our situations. We must, therefore, change the notion of limitation to frontier, and face it with persistence and diligence. Successful people exceed themselves on many levels, often even surprising themselves. The whole area of possibility thinking comes from this reframing. Where are we now and where can we be if we look forward to all our challenges as new frontiers?

Honor Your Roots

ALEX HALEY GAVE THE WORLD a wonderful gift when he wrote *Roots*. In his efforts to revere his own family heritage, Haley taught us to look for that which is unique and strong in our own ancestors and family members.

A current psychological movement includes analysis of our "dysfunctional families." People who feel injured by the events of their pasts are forming support groups to discuss their mutual concerns. Such commiseration is commendable if it leads to healing. However, if such analysis is used to justify a person's inability to succeed in life, then the whole picture needs to be reframed. We all know people who blame everybody else for their own circumstances, justifying their inability to move forward. There certainly are people who have been injured – physically, emotionally, and spiritually – by acts of cruelty committed by family members. Successful people have learned to identify these negative forces and find ways to make peace, to forgive, and to move forward.

We must honor our roots. If our backgrounds do not seem

worthy of honor, then we must grow new eyes and reframe the picture of our pasts. Each of us has the ability to choose how we look at our background and at our roots. In my seminars, I have participants draw up their family tree and locate those members of whom they are least proud. Then I have them identify at least one good trait about each that they might have inherited. What trait did that horse thief in your past have that you see in yourself? Creative marketing skills? A strong body? A keen, inventive mind? Great negotiation skills? I believe that we can choose how we look at our background. If we look for positive people, positive role models, and positive genes, we will find them. Through appreciating them, we will learn to love ourselves more.

In honoring our roots, we must learn to forgive others. There are bad people in this world – cruel, unthinking, insensitive people who hurt others. Do they mean to? I don't know. Do they enjoy it? I'm not sure. Can we improve our lives and succeed in spite of them? Of course we can. But first, we must forgive them. We must try to understand what makes them tick and attempt forgiveness. Forgiveness is not for their sake, but for yours. Once you learn how to forgive the people who have hurt you, then you can forgive yourself and move on to a complete, successful life. It takes great chutzpah to forgive the people who have hurt you and ultimately to forgive yourself.

Jay made great strides in his life when he was finally able to forgive his mother for lying to him. Doreen is trying to forgive her father and, in analyzing his roots, has learned to understand him better. As George Bernard Shaw said, "If you can't get rid of a family skeleton, you might as well make it dance."

It takes great chutzpah to move forward despite a dysfunctional, hurtful past. If you decide to take the energy you spend worrying about the past and focus it on the opportunities of the future, then you will be successful.

We learn to love ourselves when we learn to truly honor our roots. Even Marie, who was physically and sexually abused by her father, and who will probably never see him or her mother again, has learned to honor the positive part of her heritage. She knows that she has inherited her father's keen analytical and technical skills and she has put them to use in her work as a medical management consultant. She does not like all the people in her roots, but by honoring them, she honors herself. Although we may not like them as people, we need to honor our parents, our grandparents, our siblings, and the rest of our family members. Once we have learned to accept them for who they are and stop blaming them for our problems, then we can move to our next level of personal power and success.

Sylvia

Sylvia was born on December 8, 1921, to a family of immigrants who relocated from Lithuania to New York City. It was a poor, but hard-working family. Sylvia's father, Abraham (aka: "Harry" when he landed at Ellis Island), worked many jobs to support his family. He delivered milk with a horse-drawn cart and was the proprietor of a small candy store. Her mother, Ida, took care of the three children, but also helped Harry in the store and with other jobs. Life was difficult enough for the Hilners, but when the Depression hit in 1929, life became even more desperate. Harry worked so many long, hard hours that it adversely affected his health and he dropped dead of a heart attack at the age of 39. Sylvia was only 10 years old at the time.

Shortly thereafter, Ida became very ill and was later diagnosed with colon cancer. She was hospitalized at Welfare Island Sanitorium where other poor patients who had no money went for their care. Sylvia, along with her older sister Millie and younger brother Joey, visited her as often as they could. The sanitorium was an ugly place and the scenes of very sick people in pain, suffering from a wide variety of serious diseases, had a strong impact on each of Ida's children. Ida was a very proud woman who was humiliated by the way she was treated at the sanitorium. She was berated and slapped by the nurses when she became incontinent, which was, of course, a result of her cancer. The children stood by, powerless to help their mother.

Aunt Goldie, Ida's sister, came to stay with the children. She was a martyr of a woman with very strict, old-fashioned, European values who bragged to the daughters that although she was married "her breasts had never been touched by human hands."

Ida died when Sylvia was just 14. The children were orphans, now taken care of by Aunt Goldie. It was a hard life for the Hilner children. Although they had no money, they had a great deal of pride. They continued through school, working when they could and bringing all their monies into the household.

Sylvia was always compared unfavorably to her older sister Millie. Millie was the intelligent one. Sylvia was only the pretty one. In the strict European traditions, pretty is as pretty does, and the role of the parent is to make sure the pretty child does not get a "swelled head." They made sure Sylvia never got a swelled head. She was constantly told at school and at home that she was not as intelligent as her sister, and all of her needs and ideas were mocked. Upon high school graduation, she went into the work world and became a secretary. Her secretarial skills were very good. She was a fast typist with great language skills. She made new friends and those included boyfriends. In her early 20's she wanted to marry one of these very decent young men, Binny, but Sylvia could not marry because her older, more intelligent, yet less attractive, sister Millie had not married. The younger sister must wait for the older sister. Binny moved on.

During World War II, Sylvia worked for the Department of the Navy in New York City. It was interesting work, but after the war she felt she needed a change. She needed to get away from New York and her family and make her own life. It was unheard of in the early '40s for a young woman to go off on her own. However, a cousin had moved to California and Sylvia saved her money to pay a visit. It was her first big outing and opportunity to be away from the family, but it was not to be. Sylvia got appendicitis and the surgery wiped out her small savings. Back to work she went. It was now right after World War II and the troops were heading home. There had been many casualties, and the number of available, marriageable men seemed to be at an all-time low. But those who did return were anxious to marry and start their families. Millie married a war veteran who was an immigrant from Poland. Now Sylvia could also think about marriage. There were a number of suitable young men where she lived, but Sylvia was anxious to leave and start a more exciting, independent life elsewhere. Her plans to travel to California had been dashed, and she felt her life was at a standstill.

Sylvia had grown somewhat tired of attending everybody else's wedding. So when she was invited to her cousin's wedding, she went reluctantly. It was a beautiful wedding and she knew most of the guests. However, out of the corner of her eye, she spotted someone she had never seen at a family gathering before. He was not very tall, but he stood very straight. His dark, curly hair framed a face with sparkling eyes and a huge grin. He had just returned from war in the Pacific and in

Japan, and looked breathtaking in his Army uniform. When she asked her cousin who the stranger was, she replied, "He is related to the groom, he is from California, and his name is Sam."

Sam

SAM MAX KRONICK was born on March 25, 1921, in Oakland, California. He was the third and youngest son of Louis and Dora, both of whom had immigrated from Lithuania earlier in the century. Louis and his brothers were tailors by trade, but also owned a number of mercantile stores in the San Francisco Bay area of California. Louis and Dora's three sons – Gus, Milt, and Sam – had their lives ordained for them. In the eastern European patriarchal family, what the father said, the children did. All three boys went to work in the store with their mother and father. They were given no salary, but were told that whenever they needed something, just go to "Pa" and he would take care of them. There would be no independent thought, and any departure from obedience would be dealt with harshly. Sam recalls, as a young child, watching his father threaten his older brother, Gus, with bodily harm by holding him by his ankles and dangling him out the high, two-story window over the street. But Pa was not a merciless man. During the Depression, he gave bread and other household staples to the poorer families in his small community. He could be generous with those he cared for, but there would often be a price to pay later.

Sam was the youngest boy. He was born prematurely and incubated in a large cigar box placed in the oven in the kitchen. He was very special to his mother and she was the same to him. But Dora was not well. She had severe diabetes and did not take care of herself.

All three Kronick boys served in World War II: Gus in Australia, Milt in England, and Sam in the Pacific. Only in his early 20's when he entered the war, Sam was forced to grow up quickly when he encountered the horrors of combat in Mindanao and the Philippines. He watched fellow soldiers die and village people slaughtered. He dodged bullets and bombs, and his best friend died in his arms. Late one night, he was forced to kill a Japanese soldier who had, unluckily for both of them, jumped into his foxhole. These events left indelible scars on his psyche as deep as the shrapnel scars left on his back.

Sam was on a transport carrier heading toward Japan when the Armistice was signed ending the war, making his stay in Japan one of peace-keeping instead of war-making. Since he was still single and both of his brothers were safely at home, Sam was kept in Japan for a year awaiting the orders for his return back to the States. Unbeknownst to him, his mother passed away suddenly while he was still in Japan. His father and brothers made no attempt to notify him while he was gone, but waited for his return to inform him of the sad news. Sam might have been able to recover from the emotional effects of the war – although he had nightmares for years and years afterwards – but he was never able to recover from the emotional devastation wrought by learning of his mother's death so long after the fact. He is still haunted by the way his mother died, not knowing at the time whether her beloved son Sam was dead or alive.

Sam returned to the family store after his time in Japan and prepared himself to work alongside his brothers. He quickly grew restless. One day, as he was absentmindedly crossing the street a block away from the store, he was hit by a Greyhound bus and thrown several hundred yards. Luckily, Sam was in great shape from his war activities and recovered quickly.

During his short convalescence, he decided to take a trip. When the invitation came for him to attend the wedding of a cousin in New York, he decided to go. He had never been back East and the idea of traveling there and visiting relatives was of great interest.

He attended the wedding in his Army uniform. He still looked terrific and appreciated the kind words of all the friends and relatives he met there. As he was chatting with another wedding guest, he felt a tap on his shoulder. Sam spun around and gazed into the eyes of a woman he had admired from a distance, but hadn't the courage to approach. She was small in stature – only 4'11" – but outgoing, vivacious, and beautiful. None of his life experiences could have prepared him for what would happen next. Sam had just met Sylvia.

Sam and Sylvia

IT WAS A WHIRLWIND ROMANCE. Sylvia showed Sam all around New York, visiting all the tourist attractions and enjoying all the sights. She was warm and friendly; he loved animals and children. They quickly fell in love. But Sam had to return to the family store in California. They wrote letters back and forth and spoke a few times on the telephone. Apparently, the proposal of marriage happened over the telephone in a rather unromantic manner.

But all had not gone smoothly. When Sam first told his father he intended to marry Sylvia, Pa's response was, "Why would she want to marry you? Does she think you have money?" Despite Pa's protest, Sam returned to New York late in 1947, and married Sylvia on January 18, 1948.

Sylvia left her family in New York, thinking she had escaped a miserable life, and found herself in the small town of Rodeo, California, facing Pa, who would try to run their lives and ruin their marriage. Sam moved Sylvia into the rooms above the store, where Pa, Gus, and Milt all lived together. Sylvia couldn't believe this family and why the "boys," as Gus, Milt, and Sam were called, stayed so close to their father.

One month after the wedding, Sylvia became pregnant. She felt sick, lonely, frustrated, and scared. If she had had the money, she would have traveled back home and faced the mocking reprisals of her family. But she decided to stay. With great insistence and fortitude, she told Sam she would not live in this house when the baby was born. They argued and argued, but finally Sam went to his father and got permission to move into a small house across the street. But Sylvia wasn't finished. She had never really stood up to anyone before, having been the obedient daughter, sister, and now wife. But the fate of her marriage and unborn child were in her hands. Although she felt powerless to change many things, she vowed that at the birth of her child, she would change this arrangement for the better. With great courage, determination, and chutzpah, Sylvia started working on Sam to leave the family business. Sylvia vowed that her daughter would not be raised in the patriarchal environment Pa represented, and that she, Sam, and the child would have a life of their own.

Idora Kronick was born on November 19, 1948, to Sam Max and Sylvia Kronick. Yes, as you may have guessed, I am the daughter of Sam and Sylvia. With my birth was also born my mother's will to fight my grandfather for control of her family. The battles that ensued were painful and scarring, and left marks on everyone. Three years later, however, my father faced my grandfather and walked out of the family business. Old bonds were broken, but soon new bonds were formed. Pa and my mother came to an understanding which allowed us to be a family, albeit a different one from what each had expected.

My parents, through their actions, have taught me many values. It is obvious that from this background, I have the chutzpah to write about success. My parents have been married almost 50 years now, have three children, and three grandchildren. It is with great pride that I thank them for rearing me to have strength, persistence, and independence.

We learn many lessons from our parents – some good, some bad – but all children must learn to live their own lives, fight their own battles, and become successful in their own way. It is because of the chutzpah of my parents and the many lessons I learned, watching their struggles and successes, that I am able to write this book. Thank you, Mommy and Daddy. I love you.

14

TRAIT #10+:

Start Life Over in the Second Inning

"Worse than a quitter is a person afraid to begin."

It was the first inning of my son's Little League baseball tournament a few years ago. Eight- and nine-year-olds were out in the field. John was playing shortstop. The boys had worked hard to get to this point but were having a very difficult time. I, the very proud Little League mother-scorekeeper, was standing next to the coach. I could see out of the corner of my eye that he was becoming increasingly agitated and redder in the face with the dropped balls, missed throws, and other errors. The kids themselves were not doing too well, either. With every mistake, their shoulders drooped, their faces went slack, and they would not even look at the coach anymore. Finally, blessedly, they accomplished the three outs and finished the inning. As they were slowly shuffling toward the dugout, Coach Godfrey yelled, "All you guys. Over here!" I thought, "Oh, boy. Is he going to give it to them now!" All the boys came over to him with their sad faces and slumped shoulders. Coach Godfrey took his finger, stuck it in their faces, and what he said next changed their day, if not their lives.

"I don't want any of you to ever think about that inning again! As far as I'm concerned, this game starts in the *second inning.*"There was dead silence. The boys couldn't believe what they had just heard. Instead of being demeaned and insulted, they were told they had a new chance. You could see the realization coming over them and their sense of pride being restored. Their shoulders relaxed, their heads came back up, and they were ready to start their game over. They went out and played a great game. I don't remember which team won, but I know that the boys learned something very important that day – it is never too late to start life over in the second inning.

Nancy Jackson knows this. At 71 years of age, she should be retired. But not Nancy. She is now an insurance agent and has been since the age of 54 when she challenged a "good ole boy" network in the insurance industry and convinced a district manager to hire her – a woman – to be his company's first female insurance agent, and a mature one at that!

"What appears to be the end may really be a new beginning."
— POSTER

In order to be successful, you must be ready to start life over in the second inning. It takes great chutzpah to pull all 10 traits together to start over: to face your fears, be persistent, dare to dream, take risks, grow new eyes, find balance, develop humor, give back, count your blessings, and love yourself. It takes all these to start over!

Starting over is more than just making a change. It is reframing what is important to you and may include restating your values, your life philosophy, and your entire view of yourself. It is a large *reframe.*

Changing jobs is not necessarily starting over if you persist in doing the wrong things all over again. Remarriage with the same kind of person, one who brings out the worst in you, one who makes you doubt yourself and alter your values, is *not* starting over. Starting over includes a new life purpose, or a recommitment to an old, forgotten purpose which became distorted along the way. It does not mean running away from someone or something if it doesn't include reexamination of old ways.

When I started over after back surgery, it wasn't just new work in a new location (my home). It took growing new eyes to see the important things more clearly, with a new focus on my health, my friends, and my loved ones.

Lucinda

I HAD MET HER AT A BAND CAMP one summer in high school. She was from New York, as is my mother, so we became fast friends. She was tall and slim; I was short and stocky. She was a terrific flutist, coming from a family of musicians. I was a crummy drummer, coming from a family of tailors. But we laughed at the same things. We talked about boys and college and marriage and kids. We looked to the future with the naive confidence of innocent teenagers who know that bad things never happen to good people. The years went by, Lucy finished college, married, and had a daughter, Teri. More years passed.

It was a truly senseless tragedy. The driver of the car and his passenger, both of whom had been drinking, assured the sheriff that they would get off the road and wait for their friend to pick them up. It was a judgment call for the seasoned officer, one he will question for the rest of his days. The car took off back down the road and instead of pulling over as promised, sped up. There was a head-on collision. Teri was killed instantly, or so Lucy hopes. For years Lucy prayed that her daughter's death was instantaneous and that she felt neither fear nor pain in the moments before her death. The jury sided with the officer and recognized that, although he had made a mistake in judgment, he was not culpable to the family, and that Teri's death was indeed a terrible and senseless tragedy.

Teri's death almost killed Lucy. She went into a downward spiral, tormented by guilt, pain, and loneliness. Even the attention of her husband, Teri's father, did nothing to comfort her. The marriage eventually dissolved and they divorced. Lucy became a recluse and hid from everyone. She avoided all contact with her prior life, but most of all tried to avoid herself. And for a while, she was successful. Through self-neglect and self-abuse, she almost killed herself.

Last summer I was back East on business and met up with my old and dear friend, Lucy. I was anxious at first, because although I had kept in contact with her, I had not seen her in many years. It was a reunion of friends and the time apart melted away. I asked her how she was doing. She told me she was finally ok.

"I wish I could tell you that there was a stellar moment of rebirth or regeneration," Lucy said, "but that was not the case. It took years for me to come back and to start my life over. It took time, patience, and therapy for me to decide to begin again. But I'm back now." She flashed me an impish grin.

"I've been to hell and I am back. And if you don't believe me, look at the license plate on my new car." As I gazed out the window of her small but exquisite apartment, I saw the personalized license plate which had to be hers. SMILE.

"I am back now and my mission is simple. It is to put a smile on other people's faces. I know that in this solar system, the time we have on earth is miniscule, relative to all time. I know that change is constant and starting over is what we do all the time. As each cell in our body is constantly changing, so are we. I'm not sure why I am back now, but I am grateful for the second chance. I will live this life less seriously, take more of it as it comes, and look forward to the rest of it. My license plate says it all."

Many people have suffered tragedies like Lucy's. While some never recover from it, Lucy has decided to put her grieving aside and move forward. She has no fear, only hope, and a great, but weird sense of humor. No wonder I love her.

We all know people who have survived tragedies and moved on to another inning of their lives. It does not take a tragedy, however to move into a subsequent inning. It can be the result of a large reframe, the realization that your life will only improve if you take the bat in your hands and hit that ball. Sitting on the bench is easy. There is no risk of failure if you don't try. It takes great chutzpah to pick up the bat one more time, walk to the plate, face the pitcher, and swing at the ball. Lucy has decided to pick up the bat again after sitting for many years on the bench. Her new inning grew out of a tragedy. Yours does not need to. Consider the story of Alice.

Alice

ALICE ANNE MOLASKY GOULD GRAHAM MOLASKY is no stranger to starting over, as you can guess from her name. As a young girl, she wanted to become an actress. When she finally made it to Hollywood for a screen test, she failed the "casting couch." Her dark, exotic looks had made her a perfect Joan of Arc in her hometown of Dayton, Ohio, but in Hollywood, much more was expected of her. Although a young woman of only 22, she had a firm set of values and would not be part of a demeaning lifestyle. She stayed out West, put her career aspirations on hold, and married an older man – a very glamorous, charming, music conductor and composer who had been a big band leader in the 1940's. It was an exciting romance and a big wedding, which quickly resulted in the birth of three sons. Alice went to college and managed to rear her sons while earning a Master's degree in linguistics and education.

When the marriage broke up, she found herself penniless and alone to raise the children. I met Alice in 1976 when she just started as an insurance company examiner for the State Insurance Division. It was her first real job in the insurance business and she had no clue what she was doing there. She had to provide for her sons, however, so she took on the task of full-time work, surrounded by experts in law and insurance. A few years later, she married again, to a widowed rancher. Life appeared good and somewhat settled. No wonder it took her by surprise when her husband announced, after seven years of marriage, that he was in love with his young secretary and wanted out of the marriage. The divorce was ugly and prolonged, and has the distinction of going all the way to the Supreme Court of the State of Nevada for resolution. Alice was forced into the next inning of her life. She wasn't thinking straight, she says, when she enrolled in law school and moved all of her possessions into a second-floor flat in San Francisco. She started law school on the day her husband married his secretary. While the divorce lingered in the courts, Alice had little in the way of liquid assets, but a great spirit of adventure which she inherited from her two grandmothers who lived long and feisty lives. When one of them died recently at the age of 102, she was still a force to deal with!

Alice was 53 years old when she started law school. She spoke to her boys regularly on the phone and visited them as often as she could, but they were older now, much less in need of her on a daily basis, and had their own lives and families to deal with.

After Alice finished law school, a world of possibilities opened up for her. While many people her age were retiring and settling into grandmotherhood, Alice was donning tailored business suits and knocking on new doors. She found herself back at the State Insurance Division and accepted the position as insurance counsel, a position she had coveted for many years. Late in 1994, the position of Insurance Commissioner became open. "What the hell," she thought. She applied for the position and subjected herself to a new series of interviews, including those with the governor of the state. On January 6, 1995, Alice Anne Molasky Gould Graham Molasky was appointed Insurance Commissioner of the State of Nevada. "The worst part," she says, "is that the newspapers stated my age for the whole world to see." This was quite a shame, for Alice had always looked many years younger than her true age, and the announcement that she had just turned 59 was almost too much for her to bear. I, for one, had never known her age and I think she preferred it that way.

Now this is a woman of chutzpah. Having begun as an examiner in the Insurance Division, she now runs the entire department, testifies before the legislature, and regularly goes nose-to-nose and toes-to-toes with insurance leaders from throughout the world. Joan of Arc is alive and well and living in Carson City, Nevada.

"So what will be in your next inning?" I asked Alice at lunch recently. "I'm not sure," she responded demurely. "Acting, perhaps?"

You can see why Alice remains one of my heroes. Her courage to start life over so many times and to just keep on going makes it clear that starting life over in the second (or later) inning has nothing to do with age, but all to do with the gumption and gall to make a change and move forward with a new life purpose.

Many of the heroes in this book represent people who have started over with a reframed vision and such a new, improved purpose. When Marie started her life over after facing her abusive parents, it was with a new sense of worthiness. She had finally taken control of her life and demanded what was rightfully hers. When Dr. Del Snider changed careers from astronaut-aspirant to anesthesiologist, it was with a new sense of purpose, to help sick, frightened people during their trying times. Valerie had to start life over or face imminent death. She was killing herself with anorexia, using a misguided approach to gain control over her life and environment. Her second inning is a life of balance – among work, play, food, and exercise. This would not have been possible without a strong revelation and near-death experience. Her new purpose is to heal herself by helping to heal others. She has learned to give to herself first, or else she will have nothing left to give to others.

Mary Ann started life over slowly and painfully with residual brain damage from the auto accident that nearly took her life. She grew new eyes when she found that she could no longer speak at breakneck speed. Finding words for her thoughts, something she had always taken for granted, was difficult, painful, and frustrating. She had to start all over as her brain needed to rewire itself. Now she wants to share her struggles with other brain-injured people. This is her new purpose. And what gall and courage it takes to speak to audiences when speaking itself is such an effort!

When Tom surpassed the limitations imposed upon him by his doctors, he developed a new purpose also. His second inning involved teaching others the value of frontiers instead of limitations and the merits of pushing onward and upward. Norman Cousins' new purpose after surviving a usually fatal spinal disease was to help medicine grow new eyes and to prove the powerful healing effects of positive emotions on the body. Nancy Jackson, my 71-year-old insurance agent, didn't just get a new job, she got a new purpose – to serve others and herself – without fear of self-doubt or old age.

These are stories of courage, determination, individuality, renewal, and regeneration. From these stories, we learn of the importance of trait #10+, the willingness to start anew, to overcome obstacles, and to rise to our next level, whatever it is. There are many reasons for starting over. Sometimes it takes a tragedy. Other times it just requires a new view.

A New View

MY MOTHER WAS ONLY 14 YEARS OLD when her mother died. She had her whole life ahead of her. She could finish school, marry, have children, grandchildren, and enjoy life. And she did these things. She married my father, reared the three of us – her way – and seemed fulfilled.

But early in her 40's, she became moody, exhausted, and fearful. She wasn't able to articulate the reasons for her malaise until one day it dawned on her like a powerful beacon. She feared she would soon die, at the age of 46, like her mother did. This is not an uncommon psychological phenomenon. Many offspring feel they will die at the same age their same-sex parent died. Mickey Mantle, the great baseball player, who recently died at the age of 63 from liver cancer, came from a family where all the men died early, by the age of 41. He always figured the same would happen to him. He lived his life furiously because he anticipated it would be over in short order. He is quoted as saying, "If I had known I was going to live this long, I would have taken better care of myself."

When my mother surprised herself by not dying at 46, she said it was like a rebirth. What she feared so strongly – dying young and orphaning her three growing children – did not happen. Instead, she survived and then she thrived. It felt to her like a new beginning. Freed of the fear of dying, she could now live. And live she has. She loved turning 50, but enjoyed turning 60 and 70 even more. She says she now has old-age antibodies. She can say whatever she wants and nobody questions her – because she's old! Old, indeed. This woman will never be old. She is spirited and young. And she is the embodiment of chutzpah! She taught me that starting over can happen any time and that you *can* teach old dogs new tricks. This was a lesson I had to learn by myself, however, and it was not an easy one. It is never easy to start over. It is painful to face yourself, your past and your present, and intentionally rewrite your future. Let me tell you how I know.

My Lesson

About a year into my business in 1986, I was feeling overworked, uninspired, and depressed. Life felt like one big job. I was tired of working, of struggling, of worrying. All I had to look forward to was more hard work. I was a single mother, rearing a young son, attending graduate school, building my consulting and speaking business, and I was *exhausted.* I was also grieving over a failed romance. After seven years of being single, I had finally found a wonderful man and was deeply in love. But the relationship was not to be. He was fresh out of a divorce and in no emotional state to get involved.

At one point, I remember sitting in my hot tub, wondering if I should go on. This thought scared me. I am enough of a psychologist to know I was in trouble! So off to the counselor I went. And what a wise one I chose. "Idora," he asked, "If you knew you had only six months left, how would you live?"

The question was like a kick to my stomach. I almost stopped breathing as the sad realization came over me. I had gotten my life so out-of-balance by feeling depressed and worrying about the future, I had lost sight of what was truly important. The only thing that was important was the here and now. I had been wasting precious moments *now* worrying about what would or would not happen *then*. Moments were whizzing by me, ungrounded and unfocused, and I was missing the point.

The Point

THE POINT IS – if we live this moment fully, the future will take care of itself. If we live this moment fully, being true to who we are and what we believe in, we will have no regrets to cloud our future. Again, new eyes. If you knew you had only six months more to live, how would you live now? When you are able to answer that question, you can start your life over in whatever inning you choose – second, third, fourth…or even in the extra innings! Let me tell you how.

Begin With the End in Mind

GIVE YOURSELF THE SIX-MONTHS-TO-LIVE TEST. If there is any gap between how you are living now and how you would be living if the end were in sight, then STOP what you are doing now and START OVER!

This is not morbid, but truly life affirming. Unfortunately, in our culture we don't handle death very well. We don't talk about it, hoping that if we deny it, it won't really happen, not to us and not to our loved ones. So we avoid it, fear it, hide from it, fight it, then suffer grief and isolation when it does happen.

Let's face it. No one really wants to die. It's distressing for the mortal mind to contemplate its own demise. Just as the *finite* cannot conceive of the *infinite,* our minds have trouble conceiving of our own death. And, of course, the contemplation of the death of a loved one is also painful and we resist those thoughts.

Morbid thoughts? I don't think so. When we think about our lives in terms of our death, we gain an important new focus. We are mortal. We will not live forever. Whatever your spiritual beliefs, we know that our life on this earth is limited and, therefore, very precious. So how should we choose to live these precious moments?

My Tombstone Eulogy

TO EMERGE FROM that dark place in which I found myself in 1986, I decided to write my own eulogy. I got the notion from my dear friend Carol, who has planned her own final services.

Carol does funerals. As an empathetic and loving soul, Carol attends the funerals of her friends' mothers, fathers, uncles, in-laws, grandmothers, and acquaintances. She is always there to give comfort to the grieving families. As a born-again Christian, Carol feels part of her life purpose is to help others through tough times, so she goes to the funeral and partakes of the service. She has, therefore, become somewhat of an expert in regard to eulogies. She has seen many she disliked, those which were disorganized and hardly representing the life and character of the deceased. So she has planned her own.

She called me one day to tell me that the program agenda was complete. She outlined who would speak, their order of appearance, and what they would say. I didn't hear my name mentioned. "Carol," I asked, "When do I get to say my part?"

"You won't be able to, Idora, because you'll be crying too hard!"

The idea that she had everything that well planned struck me very funny. But then the practicality of it also struck me. Why should we leave the script of that last meeting of our friends and family to chance – letting strangers say generic things about us and our lives, maybe missing the most important and key points, maybe not catching our life's true essence at all?

Carol has it right. We should plan for these things like we plan for our other important ceremonies and life transitions. We would feel much more serene knowing that this final program was planned to our liking!

So I planned my own eulogy – the words I wanted placed on my tombstone. The final words which would sum up the meaning of my life. What I'd be remembered for. More accurately, what I *wanted* to be remembered for. I considered who I was, what my roles were, and what I wanted to accomplish with each. At first, I was tense and serious as I contemplated these lofty notions. But as I got into my rhythm, I started to relax and enjoy the experience. I tickled myself with some of my silly ideas. By the time I was finished, I had a smile on my face and a lightness in my spirit. I had written a masterpiece – well, maybe more of a blueprint for the masterpiece that would be my life. By articulating the desired outcome, the path was set for how to get there. If I hadn't been doing the things that would get me to my desired end, then I could start right now!

I was ready to start life over with a clearer focus and sharper purpose. I could hardly wait. It took great chutzpah to describe myself in such positive, glowing terms. But then, why not! It was my life and I could be whatever I wanted to be. My tombstone eulogy is included here for you. How do my aspirations compare with yours?

Here is my challenge to you. For those of you with great courage, a serious sense of humor, and a growing spark of chutzpah, write up your own tombstone eulogy. Describe how you want to be remembered for all the important aspects of your life – physical, emotional, social, spiritual, and the rest. Be creative, be positive, be outrageous.

It's your life. It's your ball game. Remember, those pitches ain't nothin' 'til you call 'em!

My Tombstone Eulogy

R. I. P.
Here Lies Idora Silver
She Was

◆ A self-motivated, independent, hard worker who did meaningful work which touched the lives of many in constructive, postitive ways

◆ A good daughter to Sam & Sylvia and loved them in spite of their imperfections (she, of course, had none)

◆ A devoted mother to her son John whom she showered with love and affection and asked only that he respect her and tweeze the whiskers on her chin when she was no longer able to do so

◆ A loyal friend to many, always offering a generous and nonjudgmental ear (and occasionally a generous & nonjudgmental loan)

◆ Careful in how she nourished her body and exercised it just enough to justify daily desserts

◆ A giver to her community contributing in a number of visible and invisible ways

◆ A good Little League scorekeeper

◆ A person with a big heart, an open mind, a creative spirit, and a sense of humor

SHE WAS OUTRAGEOUS!

PART III

101 Ways to Get More Chutzpah!

15

101 Ways to Get More Chutzpah!

Trait #1

1. Face your fears
2. Yell them down
3. Laugh at them
4. Overcome them
5. Do what you fear most
6. Do it again
7. Teach your butterflies to "fly in formation"

Trait #2

8. Be persistent
9. Treat your failures as successes
10. Get up one more time than you fall down
11. Keep picking up the bat
12. Keep swinging the bat
13. Take batting lessons, for Godsake
14. Try a new sport
15. Act successful
16. Just do it

Trait #3

17. Dare to dream
18. Dream big
19. Dream bold
20. "Open up your mind and let your fantasies unwind"

Trait #4

21. Take risks
22. Bet on yourself
23. Forget about security
24. Don't give up, but...
25. Don't throw good money after bad

Trait #5

26. Find balance
27. Be focused and flexible
28. Be honest and hopeful
29. Be patient and persistent
30. Enjoy everything in moderation
31. Learn what you can change and what you can't

Trait #6

32. Give and give back
33. Give money
34. Give time
35. Give attention
36. Give training
37. Give acceptance
38. Give support
39. Give truth
40. Give vulnerability

41. Give openness
42. Give love

Trait #7

43. Grow new eyes
44. Reframe the picture
45. Look at it through others' eyes
46. Redefine your past
47. Redefine your future

Trait #8

48. Count your blessings
49. Look for what's right
50. Turn negatives into positives
51. Unwrap every day as a special gift
52. List all your assets
53. Include your talents and your dreams

Trait #9

54. Laugh at life
55. Laugh through tears
56. Laugh through pain
57. Rejoice in the miracle of humor
58. Rejoice in the miracle of slapstick humor
59. Watch the Marx Brothers
60. Create humor in the workplace
    (unless this is truly a myth)
61. Practice self-deprecating humor
62. Give the world the finger (when necessary)
63. Teach others to laugh
64. Laugh at yourself!

Trait #10

65. Love yourself
66. Accept yourself
67. Accept others
68. Forgive yourself
69. Forgive others
70. Be honest
71. Be kind
72. Choose good friends
73. Be loyal
74. Trust yourself
75. Trust others
76. Celebrate your uniqueness
77. Become your own best friend
78. Befriend others
79. Do a good deed every day
80. Accomplish things
81. Stand for something positive
82. Enjoy the success of others
83. Admit your mistakes—loudly
84. Invest in yourself
85. Compete only with yourself
86. Honor your roots
87. Make your family skeletons dance

Trait #10+

88. Start life over in the 2nd inning
89. Forget a bad 1st inning
90. Develop a new life purpose
91. Allow your spirit to renew itself
92. Believe in magic
93. Believe in yourself
94. Forget your age
95. Go back to school
96. Finish that project
97. Start a new one
98. Know your values
99. Write your own eulogy
100. Write a book on chutzpah
101. Dedicate it to yourself

Bibliography

1. Anthony, Dr. Robert, *Doing What You Love, Loving What You Do,* The Berkeley Publishing Group, 200 Madison Avenue, New York, NY 1991

2. Bolton, Robert, Ph.D., *People Skills,* Prentice-Hall, Inc., Englewood Cliffs, New Jersey 1977

3. Brown, Les, *Live Your Dreams,* Avon Books, 1350 Avenue of the Americas, New York, NY 1992

4. Canfield, Jack, and Hansen, Mark Victor, *Chicken Soup for the Soul: 101 Stories to Open the Heart and Rekindle the Spirit,* Health Communications, Inc., 3201 Southwest 15th St., Deerfield Beach, Florida 1993

5. Cousins, Norman, *Head First,* The Penguin Group, 375 Hudson Street, New York, NY 1989

6. Covey, Stephen R., *The 7 Habits of Highly Effective People,* Simon & Schuster, Inc., New York, NY 1990

7. Dershowitz, Alan M., *Chutzpah,* Little, Brown & Company, New York, NY 1991

8. Dickson, Paul, *Baseball's Greatest Quotations,* Harper-Collins Publishers, Inc., New York, NY 1991

9. Dyer, Dr. Wayne W., *You'll See It When You Believe It,* Avon Books, Division of The Hearst Corporation, New York, NY 1989

10. Fulghum, Robert, *All I Really Need to Know I Learned in Kindergarten,* Ivy Books, Published by Ballantine Books, New York, NY 1988

11. Greenfield, Eloise, *Rosa Parks,* Thomas Y. Crowell Company, New York, NY 1973

12. Kubistant, Tom, *Performing Your Best,* Life Enhancement Publications, Division of Human Kinetics Publishers, Inc., Champaign, IL 1986

13. McKoron, Robin, *Eleanor Roosevelt's World,* Grosset & Dunlap, New York, NY 1964

14. McWilliams Peter, and John-Roger, *Do It! Let's Get Off Our Buts,* Prelude Press, Inc., Los Angeles, CA 1991

15. Mortell, Art, *The Courage to Fail,* McGraw-Hill, Inc., New York, NY 1993

16. Peale, Norman Vincent, *The Power of Positive Thinking,* Fawcett Crest Books, by Ballantine Books, Division of Random House, Inc., New York, NY 1963

17. Reynolds, Quentin, *The Wright Brothers,* Random House, New York, NY 1950

18. Robbins, Anthony, *Unlimited Power,* Ballantine Books 1986

19. Smith, Manuel J., Ph.D., *When I Say No, I Feel Guilty,* Bantam Books, 1540 Broadway, New York, NY 1975

20. Smith, Robert, *Pioneers of Baseball,* Little, Brown & Co., Toronto, Canada 1978

21. Thomsen, Robert, *Bill W. 50th Anniversary Edition Commemorating the 1935 Meeting Between Bill W. and Dr. Bob that Launched Alcoholics Anonymous,* Harper & Row, New York, NY 1975

22. Viscott, David, M.D., *Risking,* Simon & Schuster, Inc., 1230 Avenue of the Americas, New York, NY 1977

23. Wiener, Valerie, *Power Communications,* New York University Press, New York and London 1994

About the Author

IDORA SILVER is a speaker, trainer, and consultant who has had a number of articles published in national publications and presents a wide range of programs on professional liability, interpersonal communication, customer service, team building, and management development.

Idora Silver, herself, is an inspiration and a role model. She has overcome a number of obstacles in her life and walks her talk every day. On a daily basis, she faces her fears (checks to see if her feet are cold), works to make businesses successful and to improve the world in which she lives. She is listed in "Who's Who of Executive Women," "2000 Notable American Women," "Sterling's Who's Who," "Who's Who in the West," and "90 Movers and Shakers in the Reno-Sparks Area in the '90's." She holds the Distinguished Alumni Award from the Leadership Reno Alumni Association, and says that some of her greatest pleasures come from the scholarship programs she has instituted and helped fund. And yes, she does all this with her own style, which she calls chutzpah! She encourages everyone to look for that spark within themselves as well.

Contact Idora Silver for more information on her speaking and training programs. She can be reached at Professional Liability Consultants, Inc., 3855 Piccadilly Drive, Reno, Nevada 89509, 1-800-682-2929.

A NOTE TO MY READERS

I HOPE YOU HAVE BEEN AS INSPIRED by the stories related in this book as I have been. I know there are many more stories out there, and I would like to hear yours. If you would like to contact me with your story, including the obstacles you have overcome in your life and what you have learned in doing so, please drop me a note at:

3855 Piccadilly Drive
Reno, Nevada 89509

I would love to hear from you and possibly use your story in a presentation or publication. Thank you.